RACING *to the* TABLE

A Culinary Tour of Sporting America

RACING *to the* TABLE

A Culinary Tour of Sporting America

BY MARGARET GUTHRIE

ECLIPSE
PRESS

Lexington, Kentucky

Library of Congress Control Number: 2002103507

ISBN 1-58150-084-X

Printed in Hong Kong
First Edition: November 2002

Distributed to the trade by
National Book Network
4720-A Boston Way, Lanham, MD 20706
1.800.462.6420

ECLIPSE PRESS

a division of The Blood-Horse, Inc.
PUBLISHERS SINCE 1916

CONTENTS

INTRODUCTION

What possible connection could there be between Thoroughbred horse racing and food? Start with the basics. It seems likely that as soon as humans domesticated the horse, or even during the process, they noticed that horses liked running in groups. As humans prospered, the possibility of one's horse(s) being faster than another's was something that could be put to the test. So racing began.

England's Charles II gave racing as we know it the greatest impetus. His interest in horse racing was so keen that he set up the first race for a "Plate," instituting a royal custom that survives to this day. The Plate race he inaugurated had something else that set it apart: it was the first race with a set of rules. Since he was six-foot-two, he also inaugurated a race of three heats of four miles each in order to encourage the breeding of "stout horses."

The king got up early to watch the morning gallops and often dined with the jockeys. He sometimes served as his own jockey, winning his share of races. In 1675, when in his mid-forties, Charles won a race of three four-mile heats. There is still a race at Newmarket called the Rowley Mile that, in its way, is a tribute to Charles II. Rowley was a prolific stallion of Charles' era; because the king also sired numerous progeny, he was affectionately nicknamed "Old Rowley" by his subjects.

Charles cherished the good things in life, perhaps because he'd spent so much of his youth in exile and poverty. He loved to dine well, and his idea of economy was to reduce the number of courses at dinner. The type of food eaten then is not such as would appeal to modern palates; suffice it to say that he and the members of his court were known for setting a lavish table. Charles had a series of royal mistresses, but the one who lasted the longest was French and was reputed to set the best table.

When the English came to the New World, so did horse racing. Horse racing in the United States, or the colonies as they then were, began almost immediately in Maryland, Virginia, and the Carolinas. Men who prospered began importing Thoroughbred horses for breeding and racing. Racing persisted, flourished, and crossed the mountains to be taken up in the future states of Kentucky and Tennessee. A race might have occurred just about anywhere, quite often on the streets of town and city, to the maximum inconvenience of everyone but the participants. (Records indicate that in the

1850s winter racing took place on the frozen surface of Lake Mendota in Madison, Wisconsin. You don't want to know how cold it has to get for the ice to thicken enough to support the weight of several large horses and their riders.)

Eventually, as we became more prosperous and settled, we followed King Charles' lead and organized horse racing, giving it specific locations and sets of rules.

Horses love to run; we love to watch them. We love to eat and so do they. A winning combination, particularly since we don't eat the same things, or at least not in the same form. I did once catch my daughter feeding granola to her pony which she justified by telling me: "Goldie likes it as much as his sweet feed." At $1.79 a pound I just bet he did. If you have any doubt that horses enjoy their food, enter a barn on a cold February evening when a hot bran mash is being prepared and listen to the eager diners awaiting their meal.

C.K.G. Billings, heir to a Chicago gas company fortune, hosted a horseback dinner at Sherry's in New York in 1903.

Since the horse is an animal that in the wild survives on the move, it needs to eat more or less all the time. Once horses were domesticated, food became something earned, something to look forward to, and something to be savored and enjoyed, precisely as we humans do. What do trainers most often say of the winning horse the day after a big race? "He/she cleaned out his/her feed tub so he/she came out of the race great."

Diamond Jim Brady really cemented the relationship between Thoroughbred horse racing and good food. Diamond Jim was an owner and an enthusiastic fan of horse racing, and even more enthusiastic about dining well. His appetite was legendary. Unlike most prodigious eaters, however, Diamond Jim had a well-developed aesthetic when it came to food. He appreciated the talents of a good chef and would go to great lengths to get a recipe recreated. He once sent a friend's son to France with instructions to get a job in a certain restaurant in an effort to learn the secret of that particular chef's Sole Marguery. It was said of the high-profile gambler, "When he pointed at a

INTRODUCTION

platter of French pastry, he didn't mean any special piece of pastry, he meant the whole platter."
He was also a legendary host. To pay tribute to his horse, Gold Heels, he gave a party at which 500
bottles of champagne were served along with $40,000 worth of other delectables.

An unusual and extreme example of sharing the table occurred in 1903 when the "millionaire
horse-enthusiast" Cornelius Kingsley Garrison Billings gave a dinner party to celebrate the inau-
guration of his new stables. Described by his friends as "horse-mad," he had spent the then enormous sum of $200,000 on the stables built in what is now Ft. Tryon Park in the Bronx. The dinner
was held in the grand ballroom of Louis Sherry's establishment in New York City, which decora-
tors had turned into a "forested glade" for the event. Each guest sat atop a horse while the waiters
were attired as grooms, complete to shiny leather boots. The gentlemen dined from small trays af-
fixed to their saddles and sipped champagne through a tube that ran to the saddlebags. The menu
for that evening does not survive, unfortunately, but similar menus for similarly elegant and extravagant dinners at Sherry's do, so we know they dined well.

In 1915 Billings imported twelve yearlings from England to help improve the breed. One of
those horses was Omar Khayyam, who won the 1917 Kentucky Derby.

While entertaining among the "horse-mad" today is a bit more restrained, the hospitality remains open-handed and generous. Derby parties in Louisville are legendary, and the parties at
Saratoga in the summer fill the society pages of *The New York Times*, to cite two examples. And if
you still think food doesn't matter to the horse enthusiast, I suggest you attend the spring steeplechases in Aiken, South Carolina. There I witnessed folding tables covered with grandmama's best
damask tablecloth, crystal vases filled with flowers, silver candlesticks, and an al fresco meal that
more than measured up to its setting.

This book contains recipes from those places that cater to the racing crowd: the tracks where the
horses run, the farms where they are bred and pastured, the after-racing places where their
human entourage likes to dine or just hang out.

Recipes also come from individual breeders, owners, trainers, veterinarians — anyone involved
in the great game of Thoroughbred horse racing and in the pleasures of the table.

Because Thoroughbreds are versatile athletes, they participate in other sports. Wishing not to ex-
clude the accomplishments of these Thoroughbreds and being interested in the fare their owners,
trainers, riders, and just plain spectators and horse lovers eat, we have included recipes from the
polo fields and steeplechase races, sports at which Thoroughbreds excel.

A Note about the Recipes

First, in order to obtain the best results, read the recipe all the way through at least once. Be sure you have all the necessary ingredients and equipment on hand before you start.

If the recipe calls for fresh, don't substitute canned or frozen unless the instructions say that such substitution will work.

If a recipe calls for wine, remember Julia Child's rule: If it isn't good enough to drink, it isn't good enough to use *in* the food. The rest of the bottle is served with the meal.

If a recipe calls for heavy whipping cream, try to find cream that has *not* been ultra-pasteurized. This treatment flattens the taste and makes the cream more difficult to whip. Regular heavy whipping cream is usually available at organic grocers and some local dairies.

Try making your own stock to use in soups and stews. It's not difficult, and the difference in taste will surprise you. Also, you will note that the recipes call for unbleached flour. One of the top cooking magazines' test kitchens found that bleached flour can add a metallic taste to certain dishes.

Where possible, I strongly recommend that you use organically certified products. They have more flavor, are better for you, and give you the opportunity to support sustainable agriculture. Most supermarkets now have organically certified dairy products and a small section of organically raised produce. You will be surprised how much better the organically raised produce tastes.

It is especially important to use organically grown citrus when a recipe calls for grated zest or rind as citrus is one of the most heavily sprayed of all the fruits that come to our table.

A crew of seasoned cooks and testers has tested all the recipes in the book. Friends who range from those who can barely boil water to a professional chef and food writer have cooked, tested, tasted, commented, and where necessary, amended. I even got the doctor who restored my vision involved in testing recipes. Why not? He's a cook as well as my eye surgeon. And he's almost as good at testing recipes as he is at restoring vision.

I would like to give the last words in this introduction to Marjorie Kinnan Rawlings from her book *Cross Creek Cookery*:

"Two elements enter into successful and happy gatherings at table. The food, whether simple or elaborate, must be carefully prepared; imaginatively prepared. And the guests — friends, family or strangers — must be conscious of their welcome...At the moment of dining, the assembled group stands for a little while as a safe unit, under a safe roof, against the perils and enmities of the world...For this short time, let them eat, drink and be merry."

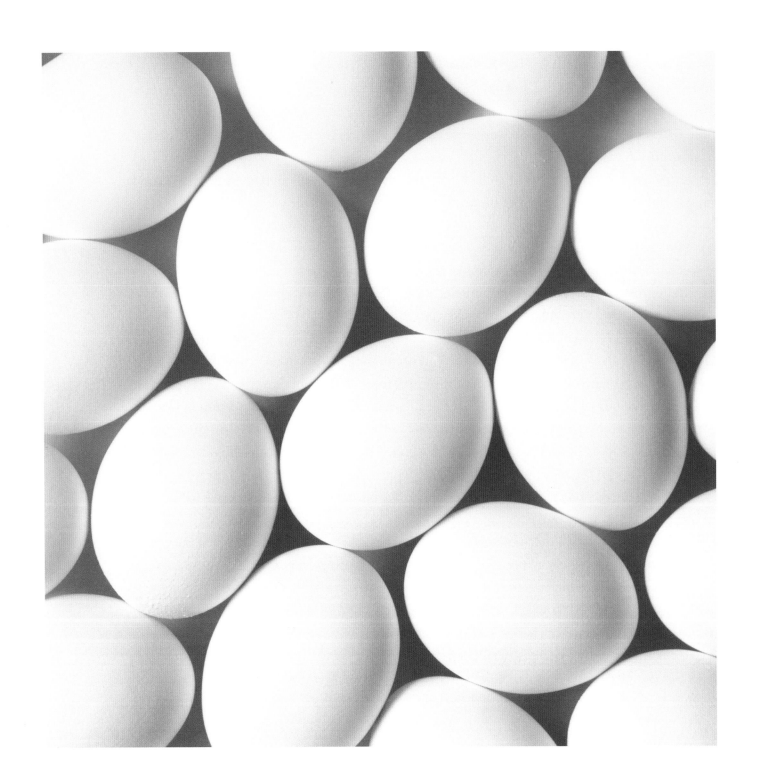

CHAPTER

1

SOUTH CAROLINA

SOUTH CAROLINA

AIKEN & HORSES, HORSES, HORSES

A iken, South Carolina, is as near to heaven as the horse lover gets while still breathing. Half the town's streets remain unpaved because horses still use them. The head of a horse adorns each street sign. There is a traffic light that controls cars going one way and horses going the other. Guess who gets the right of way.

This horse-lover's paradise lies in the western part of the state, near Augusta, Georgia. The town dates to 1835 and was named for William Aiken Sr., who was the president of the South Carolina Railroad & Canal Company. In 1836 the company constructed what was then the longest railroad in the world, running for 136 miles from Charleston almost due west to Hamburg, South Carolina. Aiken is about seventy-five miles from Charleston, or about halfway on the original line.

The railroad transformed what had been a crossroads into a bustling little town and a summer getaway for Charlestonians who wished to escape the heat and malarial swamps of the lowlands. The railroad made it an easy day's journey.

The traditions of low country cooking that coast dwellers brought to Aiken continue today. Lowlanders know how to cook. **Okra Soup** is a low country favorite and this recipe comes from the little cookbook put out by the women of Old St. Andrew's Parish Church

Horses have the right of way in Aiken.

SOUTH CAROLINA

OKRA SOUP

1 pound meaty beef soup bones

6 quarts water (about), divided

3 (10-ounce) packages frozen okra

2½ cups chopped canned tomatoes or
   10 fresh tomatoes, chopped up

2 medium onions, peeled

3 cloves

2 bay leaves

1 teaspoon dried thyme

1 (10-ounce) package frozen lima beans

1 (10-ounce) package frozen corn kernels

Salt & freshly ground black pepper

Put the soup bones in a stockpot with 3 quarts of the water and simmer until the meat is falling off. This will take about 1½ hours. If you use a pressure cooker, reduce the water to 1½ cups and cook for 20 minutes.

Combine the okra, tomatoes, onions, cloves, and bay leaves in another stockpot with 2 quarts of water.

Cut the meat into small, bite-sized pieces and add the meat and the meat broth to the vegetable mixture. Simmer about 3 hours until you have the desired thickness. Stir often. Add the lima beans and the corn during the last hour of cooking. Add salt and pepper to taste. Yield: 6 – 10 servings, depending upon appetite.

ROSE'S CORN BREAD

1¼ cup stone-ground cornmeal

1-plus cup buttermilk or sour milk

1 cup unbleached flour

2 – 3 tablespoons sugar (optional)

3 teaspoons baking powder

½ teaspoon salt

1 egg, well beaten

⅓ cup canola or vegetable oil

Preheat the oven to 350 degrees. Butter an 8x8x2" pan thoroughly.

Soak the cornmeal in the buttermilk for a half hour. This enhances the flavor. Sift in to the corn bread-buttermilk mixture the flour with the sugar, baking powder, and salt. Mix. Beat the egg, add in the oil, and stir into the batter. The batter should pour out; if not, add more buttermilk. Stir just to moisten all the dry ingredients. Batter should be lumpy.

Pour into the pan and place in the oven. Bake for 30 minutes or until top is golden brown around the edges. Yield: 4 – 6 servings.

You can also add about ⅓ cup of fresh or frozen corn to this recipe, stirring it in just before pouring the batter into the pan for baking. To serve with southwestern food, just add chopped jalapeño instead of the corn.

near Charleston, the oldest active Episcopal church in South Carolina. The little book is part of the church's fund-raising efforts. The address to buy one is given in the bibliography at the back of this book.

This soup needs to be served with a good, savory corn bread. Or biscuits.

Rose Dias worked for my family for many years, helping to raise me and my sisters. One of the most valuable things she taught me was her corn bread recipe. Since she was born on one of the islands off the South Carolina coast, the **Rose's Corn Bread** recipe belongs here. After moving north to Philadelphia, the only change she made, she said, was to add sugar. For a savory corn bread, simply eliminate the sugar. The only change I made is to use stone-ground cornmeal for added flavor.

Aiken's evolution from a temperate getaway for low country residents to a horse lover's paradise began in the 1880s when wealthy New Yorkers started migrating there in the winter, bringing their horses with them so they could continue to play polo, hunt, and steeplechase. During the town's golden era these wealthy vacationers constructed grand homes and estates that made Aiken an exclusive address. As the human population grew, so did the horse population. Gradually, Aiken became a training center for all manner of horse activities.

Curious and unable to make even a wild guess, I once asked a veterinarian there to estimate the horse population.

"Oh," he said, "at peak season I'd

Aiken is noted for its gardens and stately homes.

guess about two thousand including the children's ponies. 'Course you can have as many as a couple, three hundred coming in for one of the polo tournaments, and that boosts it."

In other words, there are a lot of horses at any given time. It's a place where on some days the human-horse ratio approaches equilibrium. The human population of the Aiken area is 25,000, so usually one horse for every twelve or thirteen people seems about right.

Aiken is a major training center for Thoroughbred racehorses. Its chamber of commerce

Future racehorses get their early schooling in the starting gate.

A lawn jockey sports the colors of Dogwood Stable, an Aiken mainstay. The training track is steeped in history.

boasts that almost every major U.S. race probably includes a horse trained in Aiken, and that's probably pretty accurate. In fact, many Thoroughbreds race for the first time in the Aiken Trials, which take place in March. Champions such as Aiken-based Dogwood Stable's Summer Squall made their first start in the Aiken Trials.

Being out in the fresh air watching others compete in a very athletic event requires plenty of fuel, both during and afterward, and no day at the races, steeplechase, or polo match

SOUTH CAROLINA

would be complete without the appropriate tailgating fare.

Mary Jane Howell is the public relations director of Dogwood Stable in Aiken. She's married to Martin Sandoval, a native of Mexico. She denies that she married Martin for this recipe for **Pico de Gallo**, but she is pretty crazy about it. Pico de Gallo, which means more or less "rooster bite," can be used as a super chunky salsa or as a salad. The idea behind

---

PICO DE GALLO

1 ripe garden tomato
1 small onion, diced
1 large bunch cilantro, chopped
Salt to taste
1 – 2 avocados, diced, depending on size and how much you like avocado
1 (6-ounce) can sweet corn, or ¾ cup leftover fresh corn

Dice the tomato; add the onion and the cilantro, which should make about 1 cup when loosely chopped. Add the avocados and corn, taste, and salt, if needed. Chill or serve at room temperature. Yield: 4 servings as salad.

BARBECUED MEATBALLS

1½ pounds hamburger	**Sauce:**
1 small can evaporated milk	**1 cup ketchup**
1 cup rolled oats or good bread crumbs	**¾ cup brown sugar**
½ cup chopped onion	**1½ teaspoons liquid smoke**
¼ teaspoon freshly ground black pepper	**¼ teaspoon garlic powder**
¼ teaspoon garlic powder	**½ cup chopped onion**
1 teaspoon chili powder	**1 (3-ounce) can tomato sauce**
1 egg	**¼ cup water**

For the meatballs: Put the hamburger in a large mixing bowl with the milk, the oats or bread crumbs, onion, seasonings, and egg. Mix well so all the ingredients are completely blended together. Using your hands, form small meatballs 2 inches in diameter by rolling between your palms. Place in a shallow oven-proof dish. Preheat the oven to 350 degrees.

For the sauce: Put the ketchup in a small mixing bowl with the brown sugar, onion, tomato sauce, and seasonings. Whisk to blend well and pour over the meatballs.

Put the meatballs in the oven and bake for 1 hour. Yield: About 50 meatballs.

the name is that it burns or stings the way a rooster's bite would. Mary Jane and Martin don't use jalapeños in theirs, but you can add them if you like. Try it their way first and see. Mary Jane even serves it at Thanksgiving dinner. And yes, of course, it goes to the races.

Barbecued Meatballs go to the races, too, and work equally well as supper at home or as a covered dish. This is easy to make, easy to serve, and delicious. Diane Smith, a local real estate agent and friend of Dogwood Stable's, always brings these to the group's table at the steeplechases.

The steeplechases are events for which a visit to Aiken is mandatory if you're a horse racing fan. The Thoroughbreds trained for steeplechasing enjoy jumping and racing over obstacles better than running around an oval track. Watching them do it is spectacular. For those who don't know a steeplechase from a flat race, steeplechasing started in England in the early

Steeplechase racing provides visual thrills and culinary delights.

19

SOUTH CAROLINA

1700s. This kind of race began impromptu "from this point to that church steeple yonder," the steeple being the most prominent point in view. The riders set out at a full gallop in a straight line for the designated steeple, taking all obstacles in stride. Or not.

Now they run on courses laid out for them, usually at distances of several miles and with a series of jumps built to test the courage and savvy of both horse and rider. Anything man can devise the horse and rider are asked to jump at full speed, often not being able to see what awaits them on the other side. Obstacles include jumps made of brush, stone walls with breakaway tops, and post and rail. Some jumps have water on one side and others have ground that falls away.

There are now some forty meets a year that range up and down the East Coast. They begin in early spring in Aiken, usually the last weekend in March, and conclude

Gardens and parks add to Aiken's aesthetic appeal.

Getting around town the old-fashioned way.

in nearby Camden in the fall with the Colonial Cup.

Thoroughbred racing is not the only kind of racing in Aiken. The town also is a major training center for Standardbred horses, as well as those that compete in eventing, dressage, and in the hunter ring. There's an annual coaching event, the kind pulled by horses, not the football kind. And every spring the steeplechase season starts here. In addition Aiken has a gem of a park in the two-thousand-acre Hitchcock Woods, a turn-of-the-century nature preserve that is ideal for horseback riding.

SOUTH CAROLINA

Polo tournaments also figure prominently on the Aiken social schedule. Aiken is one of the country's oldest polo centers, having had active polo teams since 1882. A tournament takes place the weekend of the spring steeplechases, so you can get a two for one and immerse yourself totally in horse heaven.

Another great dish, this one contributed by Sara Wood, another of the Dogwood Stable regulars, is a veteran of tailgate parties. This colorful **Wild Rice Salad** can be a meal in itself or a perfect party partner for a lot of other food at the tailgate. It's also easy to prepare and can be done ahead. This salad can be started two ways: using regular rice as the directions give here or using a boxed wild rice mix. If you choose the boxed mix, you use two boxes and eliminate the butter or margarine called for in the how-to section.

Aiken has its share of excellent restaurants, some of which cater and all of which are happy to see you after the races. No. 10 Downing Street is one of Aiken's best and is in a house, originally a small cottage, built in 1834 by the Legare family in the southern colo-

---

WILD RICE SALAD

1 cup brown rice
½ cup wild rice
5 – 6 cups chicken stock, or water
1 (10-ounce) package frozen green peas
1 yellow bell pepper, chopped
1 red bell pepper, chopped
1 bunch green onions, cleaned & sliced

1 cup golden raisins
1 cup dry-roasted peanuts, rough chopped

Dressing:
¼ cup olive oil
¼ cup champagne vinegar
⅛ cup honey
2 teaspoons curry powder

In a large saucepan, put the brown rice and 4 cups of the chicken stock or water; bring to a simmer. After 15 minutes of simmering, add the wild rice and another cup of stock or water. Simmer, stirring often, until all the water or stock has been absorbed and the rice is tender. Set aside to cool.

While the rice is cooking, thaw and drain the peas, chop the other vegetables, and prepare the dressing. The peanuts can be rough chopped best in a food processor by pulsing briefly.

Put all the vegetables together in a mixing bowl and toss gently to mix. When the rice is cooked and removed from the burner, stir the rice into the vegetables, pour the dressing over all, and stir again gently to mix. Cover the bowl with plastic wrap and refrigerate or serve at room temperature. Top each serving with the chopped peanuts or put in a bowl to pass with the salad. Yield: 10 servings.

SHRIMP PROVENÇAL WITH GOAT CHEESE

1 (16-ounce) box linguine
½ cup butter
1 medium onion, peeled & chopped
1 tablespoon chopped garlic
Kosher salt, freshly ground pepper
1 cup dry white wine
8 ounces fresh goat cheese*

2 tablespoons fresh lemon juice
36 medium shrimp, peeled, deveined,
  tails left on
1 cup seeded diced tomatoes
½ cup sliced scallions
½ cup chopped fresh basil

The goat cheese should be a fresh cheese without rind, but dry enough to crumble easily.

Start cooking the linguine according to package directions.

In a sauté pan over low heat, place the butter, the chopped onion, garlic, and salt and pepper. Cook with the lid on until the onions are translucent, about 10 minutes. Add the wine, lemon juice, and shrimp. Cook 3 minutes covered. Remove lid, stir the shrimp, add the diced tomatoes, scallions, and basil leaves, and continue cooking for another 3 – 4 minutes, again with lid on.

Drain the linguine and divide onto plates. Place the shrimp mixture on top of the linguine. Reduce the liquid in the shrimp pan by returning to burner and leaving the lid off for 1 minute. Pour reduced liquid over the servings; crumble the goat cheese liberally over each serving.

Yield: 4 servings.

---

nial style. Thomas Morgan, a British sea captain, purchased the cottage in 1870 and added two wings, turning it into a substantial house. It was placed on the National Register in 1976, remained in the Morgan family until 1985, and was completely restored and opened as a restaurant in 1989.

One of No. 10 Downing Street's signature recipes, **Shrimp Provençal with Goat Cheese**, makes great use of goat cheese, which not too many years ago was considered exotic. Now, good fresh goat cheese is available almost everywhere, and many of us can't imagine life without it. Most fresh goat cheese has a mild flavor similar to, but more interesting than, cream cheese, and it's better for you. It's infinitely useful in the kitchen and adds a piquant note to a lot of dishes.

Pork can be almost as versatile as chicken. Look what No. 10 Downing Street does with **Jerk Pork Tenderloin with Black Beans**. This makes a good, unusual dinner party dish.

SOUTH
CAROLINA

SOUTH CAROLINA

It can also be served with "dirty rice" or plain brown rice instead of beans.

No. 10 Downing Street also shared a great appetizer or something you can put on pasta as a main dish and serve with a baguette, a good green salad, and a bottle of sturdy red wine like a Cotes du Rhone or a Chianti Classico. This recipe for **Caponata** makes enough to serve a large cocktail party or at least two good-sized suppers.

From tailgating with picnic hampers to dining with china and crystal in upscale restaurants, Aiken offers food in a variety of settings. An additional way to experience the region's cuisine is in the tearoom of Old St. Andrew's Parish Church. For two weeks each spring the parish women offer an inexpensive and delicious taste of lowland cuisine. From their little cookbook, here is **Huguenot Torte**. One of the ladies of the parish assured me

---

JERK PORK TENDERLOIN WITH BLACK BEANS

3 pork tenderloins

For the beans:
  1 (8-ounce) package dried black beans
  1 small onion, chopped
  2 ham hocks
  1 teaspoon dried cumin
  4 bay leaves

For the rub:
  2 teaspoons coarse salt
  1½ teaspoons freshly ground black pepper
  2 teaspoons dried thyme
  2 teaspoons ground cumin

½ teaspoon crushed red pepper flakes
1 teaspoon paprika
½ teaspoon ground cloves
½ teaspoon freshly grated nutmeg
½ teaspoon ground allspice
¼ cup light brown sugar, packed
1 teaspoon garlic powder

Kosher salt, freshly ground pepper
¼ cup sour cream
4 chopped scallions
1 tomato, seeded and chopped

Cook the beans according to the directions on the package, adding the onion, ham hocks, cumin, and bay leaves. When the beans are cooked, remove the ham hocks and bay leaves. Discard ham hocks and bay leaves. Reserve the beans.

For the rub, combine all 11 ingredients in a small bowl. Rub generously into the pork tenderloins. Grill, turning often, until the internal temperature reaches 135 degrees. The tenderloins can also be cooked under the broiler indoors. Broil on one side about 5 minutes or until meat is browned. Turn and brown other side; then turn oven down to 350 degrees and bake 10 minutes. The meat, when sliced, should be tender, moist, and just barely pink in the middle. Remove, slice, and serve with the black beans, already prepared, and the sour cream, scallions, and tomato. Season to taste. Yield: 6 servings.

CAPONATA

2½ pounds eggplant(s)	3 pounds diced canned tomatoes
¼ cup olive oil	½ cup capers
½ teaspoon salt	½ cup minced flat-leaf parsley
¼ cup olive oil	¼ cup red wine vinegar
3 cups diced onion	½ tablespoon minced garlic
3 cups diced celery	1 (6-ounce) can tomato paste
2 cups diced red bell pepper	1 tablespoon sugar (optional)
1 tablespoon chopped fresh basil	½ teaspoon salt &
1 tablespoon chopped fresh oregano	freshly ground black pepper

Peel and dice the eggplant, sprinkle with the salt, and set aside to drain.

Put the olive oil in a heavy-bottomed large sauté pan over medium-low heat. Add the onion, celery, red bell pepper, and herbs. Cover and simmer for 15 minutes or until the onions are translucent.

Add in the tomatoes, capers, parsley, vinegar, garlic, tomato paste, and seasonings. Continue to simmer.

In a separate sauté pan, cook the eggplant in the olive oil for 5 minutes over medium heat. Add to the tomato mixture and continue to simmer for 30 minutes, stirring to make sure nothing sticks to the pan. Keep as low heat as possible to maintain a simmer. Cool and refrigerate.

Serve at room temperature with sliced baguettes or serve hot on pasta with freshly grated Parmesan or Romano cheese. Yield: 6 for dinner twice; appetizer or hors d'oeuvres for 20 – 30.

This dish freezes well. As part of testing this recipe, we froze a 1-quart container and thawed it out three months later. Exactly as it was the day we made it.

that it looks wonderful coming out of the oven, then falls flat "and looks awful, but tastes wonderful." She's correct.

Southerners love their dessert, and **Red Velvet Cake** embodies the best of Southern cooking and hospitality. Southerners love their cake and make extravagant, flavorful creations. This cake makes a spectacular addition to any tailgate party, picnic, or dinner party. If it doesn't establish your reputation as a cook to be reckoned with, nothing will. This is the contribution of the aforementioned Diane Smith, whose enthusiasm for tailgate parties is only matched by her willingness to cook for them.

Most of the food presented in this chapter is portable and will make you the hit of the

SOUTH CAROLINA

Aiken's version of the Racing Hall of Fame and Museum.

HUGUENOT TORTE

2 eggs
1½ cups sugar
2½ teaspoons baking powder
¼ teaspoon salt
4 tablespoons unbleached flour
1 teaspoon vanilla extract
1 cup chopped pecans (or walnuts)
1 cup chopped tart cooking apples
1 cup whipping cream
1 – 2 tablespoons sherry

Generously butter a 12x8x2" baking pan. Preheat the oven to 325 degrees. Chill a mixing bowl for whipping the cream.

Beat the eggs and sugar until thick and lemon-colored. Add the baking powder, salt, and flour and continue beating until well mixed. Add in the vanilla extract; blend well. Then add in the nuts and apples.

Pour into the prepared pan and bake for 45 minutes or until crusty and brown (the crust will fall). Cut into squares and serve, crust side up, with a spatula.

Whip the cream in the chilled bowl until stiff peaks form. Add sherry to taste and ladle a good dollop on each square of the torte before serving. Yield: 8 – 12 servings.

---

day. Other recipes are for foods meant to be consumed in the comfort of your own home. Keep reading to see how the rest of the country's horse racing enthusiasts dine.

RED VELVET CAKE

2½ cups self-rising flour
1 teaspoon baking soda
1 teaspoon Dutch process cocoa
1½ cups sugar
1 cup buttermilk
1½ cups canola or other good vegetable oil
1 teaspoon vanilla extract
1 teaspoon white vinegar
2 large eggs, well beaten
1 (1-ounce) bottle red food coloring

Generously butter three 9-inch round cake pans. Preheat the oven to 350 degrees. Mix all the dry ingredients in a large mixing bowl.

Put the buttermilk, oil, vanilla extract, vinegar, and eggs into another large mixing bowl and whisk briskly to mix thoroughly. When it is blended, add the food coloring and stir in to blend the color evenly.

Add the wet ingredients to the dry, using a mixer. Pour into the 3 buttered cake tins and place them in the oven. Bake for 20 minutes or until a cake tester or straw inserted in the center of the cakes comes out clean. Put the cakes on a rack and cool to room temperature.

Frosting:
1⅓ sticks butter, room temperature
10 ounces cream cheese, softened
1 pound confectioners' sugar
1½ cups chopped pecans

Topping:
½ cup chopped pecans

Put the butter and the cream cheese into a large mixing bowl. Beat well to blend and gradually sift in the confectioners' sugar, beating well after each addition. Add in the pecans last and then frost the cake, first putting the layers together with the frosting and then covering the sides and the top. Use the last half cup of pecans to coat the sides of the cake.

CHAPTER

2

LOUISIANA

LOUISIANA

"LAISSEZ LES BON TEMPS ROULER"
& THE FAIR GROUNDS

When you think about New Orleans and Louisiana, you might not think of horse racing at first. Jazz, Louis Armstrong, Mardi Gras, crawfish étouffée, gumbo, riverboats; New Orleans and Louisiana are evocative of many wondrous things. However, horse racing has been an important part of the culture of "les bon temps" for as long as good times have been in the Big Easy and its environs.

The Fair Grounds in New Orleans is America's oldest continuously operating racetrack. First laid out in 1852 as the Union Race Course, the track has been through many ups and downs. It celebrated its 130th racing season as we gathered recipes for this book.

The track suffered its first major trauma in 1862 when Union troops occupied New Orleans and halted racing. Many Thoroughbreds were confiscated and sold at auction. Shipped north, they were intended, in the words of one purchaser, "to improve the breed for the Turf." It is likely that some of those horses auctioned off, as well as those sold for "improving the breed for the Turf," were pressed into service for the Union cavalry.

During the war the racecourse became the Mechanics and Agricultural Fair Grounds, where Thoroughbred racing vied with harness, Quarter Horse, and cavalry races, as well as boxing, baseball, and bull and bear fights in entertaining the war-weary public.

At the end of the war, the Metairie Jockey Club was organized and took over the track's operation. In 1872 the Metairie became the Louisiana Jockey Club, which initiated an inaugural stakes race of two two-mile heats. In 1873 the post parade "in the French manner" was introduced, as France continued to influence life here in many large and small ways. At all American tracks now, horses and riders parade to the post "in the French manner."

Like New Orleans itself, the Fair Grounds has attracted its share of the flamboyant and the infamous over the years. In 1906 Diamond Jim Brady, the legendary bon vivant and en-

Fair Grounds racetrack in New Orleans embraces the character of its hometown.

33

Diamond Jim Brady raced horses at the Fair Grounds.

thusiastic racehorse owner, was on hand to see North Wind breeze home the winner in the feature race at odds of 200-1. It's not recorded on which horse Diamond Jim had placed his money, but since he liked to bet the way he liked to eat, it's unlikely the odds for North Wind would have remained so high had Brady bet on him.

Twenty years later Colonel E.R. Bradley, another enthusiastic owner and the breeder of five Kentucky Derby winners, including Burgoo King, purchased the Fair Grounds and ran it for six years until his retirement.

Between then and now the Fair Grounds knew many more owners and turbulent episodes, including a fire in the early 1990s that resulted in a new clubhouse and grandstand. From some lean years it has emerged as a premier winter racing venue, with purse money boosted by inter-track wagering and video poker revenues, and a track surface that many trainers describe as the best. Many good horses emerge from winter racing in New Orleans to capture the sport's biggest prizes.

As three-year-olds, Risen Star and Grindstone won the Louisiana Derby and went on to racing fame. Risen Star won both the 1988 Preakness and Belmont stakes and Grindstone took the 1996 Kentucky Derby. The Louisiana Derby carries a purse of $750,000 and is a serious step on the road to the Triple Crown races, attracting top-flight three-year-olds.

OYSTER & ARTICHOKE SOUP

3 tablespoons butter
2 cups chopped onion
2 cups chopped green onions
2 cups chopped green peppers
1 cup chopped leeks
2 cups canned artichoke hearts, drained
2 teaspoons roasted garlic
½ cup dry vermouth
1 cup oyster liquid
2 cups raw oysters
1 teaspoon dried thyme
1 bay leaf
1 quart heavy cream
Salt & pepper to taste

Roux to thicken:
3 tablespoons butter
3 tablespoons flour

In a deep, heavy-bottomed saucepan, melt the butter and sauté the onion, green onions, peppers, and leeks until the onion becomes translucent, about 5 – 10 minutes. Add the artichoke hearts and the roasted garlic; cook, stirring gently another 3 minutes. Add the vermouth and the oyster liquid. Reduce at a simmer for 2 minutes; then add the oysters, the herbs, and the heavy cream. Cook on low heat for 10 minutes. Meanwhile, in a separate saucepan melt the remaining 3 tablespoons of butter; then add the flour. Stir over medium heat until the mixture darkens a bit. Add to soup. Season to taste and serve. Yield: 5 very rich servings.

The Fair Grounds, being in New Orleans, has to have good food. Look at the competition from the city's many, many fine restaurants. Food is a way of life here; people live to eat in southern Louisiana. Think of the heritage: French, Creole, Cajun, and a sprinkling of Caribbean, South American, Italian, and Spanish. Right near the Gulf of Mexico, New Orleans naturally takes advantage of the seafood. And since the weather can be damp and sometimes a little chilly, Chef Pete deMarcay of the Fair Grounds cooks up

Local hero Risen Star won the 1988 Louisiana Derby.

this **Oyster & Artichoke Soup** to make you feel warm and give you comfort when your horse wasn't in the mood to run.

Seafood Casserole deMarcay from Chef deMarcay takes its place among the most elegant of dishes for dinner. Serve it with rice, egg noodles, mashed potatoes, or just about anything good to soak up the sauce. It can also be served in individual ramekins for a special presentation. Can you tell you're near the Gulf of Mexico?

Tom David has been a track veterinarian in Louisiana since 1968 when he started at Evangeline Downs in Lafayette. "This was certainly the greatest culture shock I had ever experienced," he says of his move from the tracks around Miami, Florida, to southern Louisiana. "The Cajun trainers were a little skeptical of an outsider, especially one that would move from Miami, Florida, to Lafayette, Louisiana." Working for the leading train-

SEAFOOD CASSEROLE deMARCAY

2 tablespoons butter
½ cup diced onion
½ cup diced red or green bell pepper
½ cup finely chopped green onion
1 pound medium shrimp, peeled & cooked
1 tablespoon minced garlic
1 cup finely sliced fresh mushrooms
1 cup heavy cream

½ teaspoon dried basil
½ pound lump crabmeat

For the roux:
  2 tablespoons butter
  3 tablespoons unbleached flour

½ cup grated or crumbled mozzarella cheese
Salt & pepper to taste

Sauté the onion, bell pepper, and green onion in the 2 tablespoons of butter in a heavy sauté pan over medium heat. Cook until the onions are translucent, 5 – 10 minutes. Add the shrimp; cook for 5 minutes. Sprinkle the minced garlic over the shrimp and stir in. Add the fresh mushrooms; cook for 3 minutes or until the mushrooms begin to give up their juices; then add the heavy cream and the basil. Stir to incorporate. Simmer on low for 3 minutes. Add the lump crabmeat and stir in. In a separate pan make a light roux with the remaining butter and the flour; add in a bit at a time until the sauce thickens. Season with salt and pepper and put in casserole dish. Sprinkle the mozzarella cheese on top and bake 5 minutes or so at 350 degrees, just until the cheese melts. Do not brown. Yield: 6 servings.

A tester suggested adding a bit of sherry to this casserole. If you like the affinity between crab and sherry, go ahead and add a bit of it when finishing the sauce and before sprinkling on the cheese and baking.

er, Pola Benoit, helped David vanquish any skeptics and soon he had a flourishing practice. But that was only part of the picture: "In that environment, if food didn't become a major part of your life, your taste buds were dead."

So began Tom David's culinary education. "At Evangeline there was always someone cooking at their barn, and on dark days (days

Black Gold, who won the 1924 Kentucky Derby, had New Orleans ties.

LOUISIANA

CHICKEN-SAUSAGE GUMBO

1 chicken (3 – 4 pound), quartered

1 onion, cut in quarters

2 – 3 celery stalks

Several parsley stems*

10 peppercorns

2 pounds Andouille sausage**

For the roux:

¾ cup vegetable oil

¾ cup flour

1 teaspoon black pepper

2 onions, chopped

1 green bell pepper, cleaned and chopped

1 cup chopped celery, chopped

1 (6-ounce) can tomato paste

1½ teaspoons salt

¼ teaspoon red pepper flakes

4 bay leaves

¼ teaspoon allspice

½ teaspoon dried thyme

Tabasco® sauce or hot sauce to taste

¼ cup chopped Italian flat-leaf parsley

1 small bunch green onions, cleaned and chopped

Use the parsley stems from the chopped Italian parsley added later in the recipe.

*** Andouille sausage may not be available in your area. Italian spicy sausage works on the East Coast. You need a sausage with a bit of bite.*

Place the chicken in a large, heavy-bottomed stockpot and add 2 quarts of water. Add the quartered onion, celery stalks, parsley stems, and peppercorns. Bring to a boil and simmer for 30 minutes until the chicken is tender. Turn off, remove the pot from the burner, and allow the chicken to soak in the broth for another 30 minutes. Remove chicken, skin, de-bone, and chop meat into chunks. Strain and reserve the stock.

Sauté the sausage in the pot in a small amount of oil; remove the sausage when browned and add vegetable oil until you have ¾ cup. Add the teaspoon of black pepper and the ¾ cup flour. Stir the flour and oil together, cooking over low heat to make a roux. Continue cooking and stirring until the roux is pecan-brown.

When the roux is ready, add the chopped onions, celery, and green pepper, cooking over medium heat until the vegetables soften. Add the tomato paste and 1 cup of the reserved stock, stirring well to blend all the ingredients together. After about five minutes, add the remaining seasonings and the rest of the reserved stock. Simmer, partially covered, for 1 hour. Add the chopped chicken and cooked sausage back to the pot and continue cooking for another 30 minutes. Keep the fire low to avoid scorching or sticking. Remove from heat. Adjust the seasonings to taste and add the chopped parsley and chopped green onions and allow to set for 15 – 20 minutes before serving over cooked rice. Yield: 6 – 8 servings, depending upon appetite.

SHRIMP & EGGPLANT CASSEROLE

2 pounds medium-sized shrimp, cleaned
   & deveined
3 medium eggplants
2 tablespoons unsalted butter
2 tablespoons olive oil
2 medium onions, chopped
½ cup chopped celery
1 medium green bell pepper, chopped

3 cloves garlic, minced
¼ cup minced Italian flat-leaf parsley
1 teaspoon fresh lemon juice
Salt, pepper, red pepper flakes to taste
2 eggs, well beaten
1 cup Italian (seasoned) bread crumbs
¼ cup freshly grated Romano cheese

Shell, clean, and devein the shrimp. Set aside. Preheat the oven to 350 degrees. Butter an oven-proof casserole or baking dish.

Peel the eggplant and cut into cubes, discarding those that are all seeds as they will be bitter. Soak the cubed eggplant in salted water for 30 minutes. Put the eggplant and water in a saucepan and bring to a simmer. Cook at a low simmer for 30 minutes or until the eggplant is tender. Drain in a colander.

Add the butter and oil to a heavy-bottomed sauté pan and cook the onions, celery, green pepper, and garlic until the vegetables are soft. Add the shrimp, parsley, and lemon juice and cook for 3 – 5 minutes until the shrimp turn pink. DO NOT OVERCOOK the shrimp or they will be rubbery.

Slightly mash the eggplant and add to the shrimp and vegetable mixture and season to taste. Fold in the beaten eggs and about half the bread crumbs. Place the mixture in the buttered oven-proof dish; top with the remaining bread crumbs and grated Romano cheese. Bake for 30 minutes. Remove and serve. Yield: 4 – 6 main dish servings.

---

when the racetrack is closed to the public) there were cookouts at local farms and homes." He began cooking when he moved to a track near Shreveport and missed the Cajun and Creole cooking of the southern tracks. He enrolled in evening cooking classes when he moved to New Orleans and cooked with well-known Creole chef Leon Soniat, whose book, *La Bouche Creole*, David considers an excellent reference. In all of this learning and tasting and eating, David learned the "holy trinity" of both Cajun and Creole cooking: celery, onions, and green pepper. And he learned to make roux, that magic blend of flour and oil cooked slowly until it caramelizes and which is the basis of many Cajun recipes.

The trick with roux is attention, stirring, and patience. Try your hand at making roux as you prepare David's **Chicken-Sausage Gumbo**. Serve the gumbo with a good crusty bread and a tossed green salad and enjoy this perfect example of the importance of *bon appetit* in southern Louisiana.

LOUISIANA

Racing at the Fair Grounds is some of the most competitive around.

FAIR GROUNDS CRAWFISH PASTA

Pasta of your choice
1 pound crawfish tail meat
2 tablespoons olive oil
1 cup chopped onion
1 cup chopped red or green bell pepper
1 cup chopped green onion

1 tablespoon minced fresh garlic
1 teaspoon dried basil
1 tablespoon flour
2 cups heavy cream
¼ cup freshly grated Parmesan or
   Pecorino Romano cheese

Cook the pasta according to package directions.

While the pasta cooks, in a large sauté pan put the olive oil, onion, and bell pepper. Cook the vegetables over medium-low heat until the onions are translucent, about 10 minutes. Add in the crawfish meat, green onion, and garlic; sauté another 3 minutes. Sprinkle the mixture with the flour; stir in gently. Fold in the heavy cream. Cook for 2 minutes and watch carefully. Do not allow it to boil. Remove the pan from the burner. Add the basil and season to taste with salt and white pepper.

Drain the pasta, place on serving plates, spoon the crawfish over, sprinkle with the freshly grated cheese, and serve.

Yield: 2 servings.

SLOW-ROASTED DUCK WITH ORANGE-SHERRY SAUCE

2¼ pounds yellow onions,
  peeled & coarsely chopped
¼ pound (1 stick) unsalted butter, melted
2 medium red bell peppers
2 medium carrots, peeled & julienned
2 cups freshly squeezed orange juice
1 cup sherry

2 (5-pound) ducks, rinsed & patted dry
Salt & freshly ground black pepper
4 large fresh rosemary sprigs
½ cup soy sauce
4 ounces small oyster mushrooms, trimmed
2 tablespoons unsalted butter
4 fresh chives, cut in 1-inch lengths

Preheat the oven to 500 degrees. In a large bowl, toss the chopped onions with the melted butter. Season the ducks inside and out with the salt and pepper and place 2 rosemary sprigs in each cavity. Tightly pack each cavity with the onions and set the ducks in a large roasting pan. Roast the ducks at 500 degrees for 10 minutes.

Lower the oven temperature to 300 degrees and loosely cover the pan with foil; roast the ducks for about 40 minutes per pound or 4⅓ hours for 5 pounders, draining off the fat every hour.

Roast the peppers directly over a gas flame until charred all over. Place peppers in a paper bag for 10 minutes to steam; peel and remove the seeds; then cut into strips. (If you don't have a gas stove, you can cut the pepper into large strips, put them under the broiler, skin side up, broil until the skin chars, and then pop them into the paper bag.)

Blanch the carrots in boiling water for 1 minute and drain; put aside with peppers.

Discard the fat from the roasting pan; add the orange juice, sherry, and soy sauce and roast ducks, uncovered, for another 30 minutes. Transfer the ducks to a warmed platter and allow to cool slightly. Pour the pan juices into a heavy-bottomed saucepan, discarding any pieces of duck skin. Skim the fat off the sauce and bring to a boil over medium-high heat. Reduce to 1½ cups of liquid, strain, and return to saucepan.

Quarter the ducks; discard the onions and rosemary. Rewarm in a low oven.

Sauté the oyster mushrooms in the 2 tablespoons butter. Add the carrots, peppers, and the sauce; salt and pepper to taste.

To serve: Place some of the sauce on the plate with pasta or shoestring potatoes; place duck on top, and then garnish with vegetables and chives. Pass the extra sauce in a sauce boat. Yield: 4 servings.

Although he doesn't say so, David's recipe for **Shrimp & Eggplant Casserole** has all the makings of a perfect Sunday dish, whether brunch or supper. It would be easy to carry somewhere and complement with good bread, salad, and wine for a complete meal. It would add a lot to a covered dish or potluck meal anywhere.

You can't have a Louisiana chapter in a cookbook and not have a recipe for crawfish any more than you can have a Maryland chapter without a crab recipe of some kind. Go to the Fair Grounds for its **Crawfish Pasta** or make it at home, but try it somehow, someway. Crawfish is available at some supermarkets at the fish or meat counter, sometimes by spe-

This historic bell summons horses to the post at race time.

cial order, and in some gourmet groceries. In most of the country crawfish come frozen.

Gabrielle's Restaurant, named for chef/owner Greg Sonnier's daughter, opened in 1992 and has been busy ever since. The acclaimed restaurant is a favorite with Fair Grounds racing fans, as well as the Big Easy's other residents and visitors. Chef Sonnier shows his Creole roots but manages a lighter touch with his culinary creations. He sent us his recipe for **Slow-Roasted Duck with Orange-Sherry Sauce**, which, unlike most Cajun and Creole dishes, has no roux.

Chef Sonnier provided us with a delicious oyster dish as well.

Oysters and artichokes seem to be a marriage made in New Orleans. One tester says, "This makes your kitchen smell so good!" She also tested it twice, curious to see how it would turn out using a jar of artichokes instead of fresh ones and putting it all in one dish instead of indi-

OYSTERS GABIE

1 lemon, halved
4 tablespoons olive oil
2 large artichokes
4 ounces pancetta, finely diced
1 tablespoon butter
¼ cup chopped green onions (white part only) or shallots
1 tablespoon minced fresh garlic

2 tablespoons minced flat-leaf parsley
Juice of 1 lemon
¼ cup plus 2 tablespoons dry bread crumbs
¼ cup plus 2 tablespoons freshly grated Parmesan cheese
16 – 20 large oysters, liquor reserved
Salt & freshly ground black pepper to taste

Bring a large pot of water to a boil. Place the halved lemon and two tablespoons of the olive oil in the water. Add the artichokes and cook until tender, about 20 minutes. To test for doneness, remove one of the artichokes from the water and pull off one of the leaves around the base. If it comes away easily, the artichoke is cooked.

Drain and cool. Pull off the leaves and scrape off the pulp at their bases. Dig out the 'choke with a spoon and dice the remaining hearts. Set aside with the scraped pulp.

Preheat the oven to 450 degrees. In a medium sauté pan or skillet, heat 1 tablespoon olive oil and cook the pancetta until it browns; add the remaining tablespoon of olive oil and the butter. Sauté the green onions or shallots, garlic, and parsley until tender, about 3 – 4 minutes. Add the diced artichoke hearts, pulp, and lemon juice. If the dressing looks too dry, add a little oyster liquor to moisten. Sauté for about 2 minutes more. Adjust the seasoning to taste. Remove from the heat, add ¼ cup of the bread crumbs and ¼ cup of the cheese and toss lightly.

Place 4 – 5 oysters in each of 4 individual casseroles. Top with the artichoke dressing. Sprinkle with the remaining bread crumbs and cheese. Bake until browned, about 10 – 15 minutes. Serve with hollandaise sauce over the dressing.
Yield: 4 servings.

HOLLANDAISE SAUCE

2 egg yolks
2 tablespoons white wine
1 tablespoon fresh lemon juice
Pinch of salt
Pinch of cayenne
1 cup warm clarified butter*
Warm water as necessary

Clarified butter is the clear part of the melted butter poured off and used in sauces.

In a double boiler, over simmering water, whisk the egg yolks, wine, lemon juice, salt, and cayenne until thick, about 5 – 6 minutes, being careful not to overcook the eggs. Add the warm butter in a thin stream, continually whisking until all the butter has been incorporated. If the sauce is too thick, add warm water 1 tablespoon at a time. Adjust the seasoning and serve. Yield: 1¼ cups.

WILD BLUEBERRY SHORTCAKE

Biscuits:
2½ cups unbleached flour
¼ cup sugar
1½ tablespoons baking powder

¼ teaspoon salt
2 tablespoons margarine*
8 tablespoons cold, unsalted butter
1 cup milk

* Select the margarine carefully; one made from pure soy with no additives works best.

Preheat the oven to 400 degrees. Mix together all dry ingredients; cut the butter and margarine into the flour mixture until the mixture resembles coarse meal. You can use two knives, a pastry blender, or put the ingredients in a food processor and use several short pulses to cut the butter into the flour mixture.

Make a well in the center of the flour-butter mixture and pour the milk into the well. Blend the dough lightly until completely mixed. Turn out on a floured board; knead 3 – 4 times, and with a well-floured rolling pin, roll out dough to ¾-inch thick. Using a 2-inch round cookie or biscuit cutter, cut out biscuits. Place on an ungreased baking sheet and brush the tops with milk. Place in the oven and bake for 15 – 18 minutes or until the biscuits are golden brown. Yield: 8 – 10 large biscuits.

Berries:
2 quarts blueberries
2 tablespoons fresh lemon juice
¼ cup fresh orange juice

1 tablespoon vanilla extract
1 cup sugar, more or less, according to taste or sweetness of berries

---

Mix the berries with the juices, vanilla extract, and sugar. Toss to blend and get the berry juice running a little. Refrigerate for 1 hour before serving. Do not make too far ahead.

Whipped Cream:
3 cups heavy cream**

¾ cup sugar
1 tablespoon vanilla extract

** Try to find heavy cream that has NOT been ultra-pasteurized. It tastes better and whips better.

Whip the cream slightly; then add sugar and vanilla and continue to whip until soft peaks form. Do not overwhip! (You get very sweet butter if you do.)

To serve: With a fork, split the biscuit in half; butter and toast biscuit; place the bottom half, buttered side up, on the plate; spoon some berries and juice onto biscuit; place the other half on top and spoon more berries on top. Spoon a generous amount of whipped cream on top of it all and serve immediately. Yield: 8 – 10 servings.

Alice Hebert's fig cake is a favorite at potlucks.

vidual casseroles. Still wonderful, she reports, but it takes the full fifteen minutes in the oven.

Oysters Gabie, also named for Sonnier's daughter, and the accompanying **Hollandaise Sauce** are guaranteed to make your reputation as a culinary expert. And it's not difficult to do, a bit time-consuming perhaps, but *pas dificile* as they would say in N'Awlins.

For dessert, Chef Sonnier offers his

HEBERT FAMILY'S FIG CAKE

2 cups sugar
1 (8-ounce) stick butter at room
  temperature
2 eggs, room temperature
1 cup milk
2 teaspoons baking soda
1½ teaspoons ground cinnamon
1½ teaspoons ground ginger

2½ cups unbleached flour
2 cups fig preserves
1 cup chopped pecans

Glaze (optional):
  1 cup sifted confectioners' sugar
  1 teaspoon almond extract
  ¼ cup hot water

Preheat the oven to 350 degrees. Generously butter and flour a bundt or tube pan. In a large mixing bowl beat the butter with the sugar until light and fluffy. Beat in the eggs. Sift together all the dry ingredients.

Add in the milk and sifted dry ingredients alternately, beating after each addition. Once all the milk and all the sifted ingredients have been incorporated, add the fig preserves and chopped pecans. Stir to blend well. Pour into the prepared pan. Bake for about 55 minutes or until a toothpick or cake tester inserted in the middle comes out clean. Remove from oven and place on rack. Cool to room temperature.

After the cake has cooled, it may be glazed, if desired. Beat the hot water and the confectioners' sugar together, adding in the almond extract. Spread on top of the cake. Place whole toasted pecans in a ring on top of the cake. Allow to cool and serve. Yield: 12 servings.

FIG PRESERVES MADE FROM DRIED FRUIT

2 (1-pound) packages of dried figs
(stems removed and chopped finely)
Juice and finely grated rind of one untreated orange
(meaning unsprayed fruit)
¼ **teaspoon cinnamon**
¼ **teaspoon nutmeg**
One pinch of cloves
1 pound pre-warmed sugar

Combine all ingredients except sugar in a large pot; cover with water, barely, and bring to boil. Slow boil for 20 – 30 minutes until the fruit has a thick porridge-like consistency. Stir in the pre-warmed sugar, having turned down the heat, stirring till dissolved.

Boil 10 – 15 minutes until it attains a jelly-like consistency. Stir when necessary. Remove from burner; remove any foam that has gathered. Pour into pre-warmed, clean, and dry jars and close tops tight. Let the jars cool and store a few days in a cool, dark, and dry place before opening.

If you use fresh fruit, 2 pounds fruit to one pound pre-warmed sugar. The preserves should be used within 3 months due to the relatively low sugar content. Over-ripe fruits should not be used for preserves.

patrons this rich, very American dessert, **Wild Blueberry Shortcake**. He uses blueberries for his short-cake, but you could easily substitute any firm berry such as strawberries or even peaches and nectarines in season. Or you could do a red, white, and blue dessert using both blueberries and strawberries, or blueberries and red raspberries. The point is to use the freshest, most local fruit you can find. This is American cooking at its very best and showiest.

For another dessert option, try Alice Hebert's **Fig Cake**, which is a great take-along and holiday cake. Alice and Doris Hebert live in Carencro, a small town in southern Louisiana near Lafayette that is home to many in the racing community. Doris is a trainer on the circuit there and known to just about anyone who has anything to do with racing at the Fair Grounds. When Alice married Doris, she got some family recipes as part of the bargain, and this fig cake is one of them. She says people ask her to bring the fig cake whenever there's a potluck.

One of our testers made her own **Fig Preserves from Dried Fruit** for this cake, as she couldn't find any in the markets in Hamburg, Germany, where she lives. She reports her cake was wonderful. This cake can easily become part of a family holiday tradition. I took it to a Christmas dinner at my sister's house. Appropriately dressed in a ring of holly, it was a huge hit and a lot easier than plum pudding.

No cookbook about any kind of American cooking can hold its own without a cookie recipe or two. And it should have a cookie that's a little intriguing, that people haven't seen before, like these fig cookies from Alice Hebert.

When testing them, tasters guessed everything from orange marmalade to peach preserves and most were amazed to hear the cookies were made with fig preserves. Maybe because we grew up thinking there's only one kind of fig cookie. This recipe for **Fig Cookies** makes very soft dough, so it's important to chill it in the refrigerator for easier handling. Soft dough makes soft cookies, so it's equally important to leave the cookies on the baking sheet or parchment paper for a few minutes to set up before removing the cookies to the cooling rack.

Louisiana, with its culinary and racing histories developing side by side, has given us a distinctive cuisine and a major component of our racing heritage. Quite a contribution.

The downtown New Orleans skyline looms beyond the Fair Grounds.

ALICE HEBERT'S FIG COOKIES

¾ **cup butter or margarine**	½ **teaspoon nutmeg**
2½ **cups sugar**	1 **teaspoon cinnamon**
3 **eggs, room temperature**	1 **cup shredded coconut**
3½ **cups unbleached flour**	2 **cups fig preserves**
1 **teaspoon baking powder**	2 **cups chopped pecans***

* Lightly toast the pecans before adding to the dough for a nuttier, more intense flavor.

Beat the butter and sugar together until light and fluffy. Add the eggs and continue beating. Sift the flour with the baking powder, nutmeg, and cinnamon. Add the sifted dry ingredients into the batter and beat to blend well. Add in the coconut, fig preserves, and chopped pecans. Stir to blend all the ingredients evenly throughout the dough. Cover the bowl with plastic wrap and chill in the refrigerator at least for 1 hour.

Preheat the oven to 350 degrees. Butter two cookie sheets thoroughly or line with parchment paper. Drop the cookie dough by teaspoonfuls about 2 inches apart on the cookie sheets. Place in the oven and bake for about 15 minutes or until just brown around the edges. Allow cookies to cool on the cookie sheet for five minutes before removing. Yield: 90 cookies.

CHAPTER

3

FLORIDA

FLORIDA

CALDER RACE COURSE, GULFSTREAM PARK, & OCALA

Florida can seem like another country to the casual visitor. The climate is tropical, as are the vegetation and spectacular sunsets. Even before the state's Thoroughbred breeding industry became as big and active as it is, East Coast and Midwest stables raced at Florida tracks during the winter. Hialeah, which recently closed, was the destination for many of Thoroughbred racing's legendary stables. Calumet Farm, Darby Dan Farm, the Whitney stable, Greentree Stable, and the King Ranch competed with one another there during racing's heyday. Major races were broadcast on the radio, and fans turned out regularly by the tens of thousands for the big races. While getting fit for spring and, hopefully, winning races, the equine athletes gave their owners, trainers, exercise riders, grooms, and jockeys the chance to bask in the sun and taste tropical cuisine.

Year-round racing was inevitable as Florida drew in more and more tourists and new residents, many of them Cubans escaping Castro. As the population grew more diverse, so did the food.

Florida's cuisine is made up of dishes from the South, Cuba, and the Caribbean as well as some fare indigenous to the area. Florida is the only part of the country where alligator is on the menu in many restaurants, and not just those given to exotic fare. From *Cross Creek Cookery*, a 1942 cookbook by Marjorie Kinnan Rawlings about living, cooking, and dining with friends in Florida, comes this advice:

"Steak from the tail of the alligator is truly delicious. It is like liver or veal (which it resembles in texture and coloring) in that it must be cooked very quickly or for a very long time." She gives two recipes, one short and one long, for preparing this delicacy. Since fresh alligator is not universally available, we'll forego the recipes and say, if you want to taste it, you'll have to go there.

Florida is a major racing center and second only to Kentucky as a producer of Thoroughbreds.

FLORIDA

During its heyday Hialeah drew most of the prominent stables from the East Coast.

As Florida became more the mecca for Thoroughbreds in the South, the region around Ocala soon was recognized as a perfect place to breed and raise Thoroughbreds. A booming industry soon developed on the rolling hills north-central Florida. Along with the

Thoroughbred farms came the ancillary businesses associated with the breeding of racehorses, such as bloodstock agents.

Bloodstock agents make their living putting people together with horses. If you suddenly get the urge to own racehorses or get involved in breeding them, a *reputable* bloodstock agent is the person to see. Find someone in the industry whom you trust because bloodstock agents come in all moral fibers. A good one can greatly aid the process and ensure that you don't fall out of love precipitously with the sport of horse racing.

Bob Cromartie

Besides being a highly reputable and longtime bloodstock agent, Bob Cromartie is known for his hospitality and prowess at the stove. From Bob we received this recipe for **Scottish Red Cabbage** that shows off his heritage to perfection.

Scottish red cabbage would go beautifully with grilled steak, lamb, or pork chops. There was no accompanying note to say what Bob serves with his, so we're using our own taste buds here.

Ocala, where Cromartie lives, also has its share of good places to eat. One of them is Nonnie's Stone Oven, owned by Charlie Deliberio, who says the restaurant takes his mind off the horse business, in which he's also involved. He enjoys serving his grand-

BOB CROMARTIE'S SCOTTISH RED CABBAGE

1 large head red cabbage, julienned
4 tablespoons butter
½ cup turbinado sugar (a partially refined sugar, light brown in color and similar to demerara)
½ teaspoon salt
2 teaspoons Beau Monde seasoning*

* Beau Monde seasoning is a combination of salt, crushed celery seed, and dehydrated onion.

Quarter the head of cabbage. Peel off the tough outer layer of leaves; cut out the tough stem. Slice the cabbage into julienne strips no wider than ⅛ inch.

In a large sauté pan, melt the butter. Mound the cabbage on top of the melted butter. Sprinkle the sugar, salt, and Beau Monde seasoning on top and shake the pan a little so the seasonings shake down into the cabbage.

Place on very low heat and cover; cook about 15 – 20 minutes or until a significant amount of water cooks out of the cabbage. Turn heat up to high and stir continuously until the cabbage is tender. Serve at once.
Yield: 4 servings.

mother's great recipes to an appreciative public — mostly other horse folk. Here's one that's easy, delicious, and can be put together in about thirty minutes, so it's great for weekday nights.

Penne with Vodka Cream Sauce can be prepared as a casserole and gently reheated. Simply put the drained penne pasta in a large, two-quart casserole and pour the sauce on top. Cover and refrigerate for later serving. Reheat in a low oven (175-200 degrees), covered, or in the microwave. Remember the freshly grated Parmesan cheese and the chives. Serve with good crusty bread, a Chianti Classico, and a salad.

While Ocala is a wonderful horse town, there's no racetrack there. For racing and wagering you'll have to head to Tampa or South Florida.

Miami's Calder Race Course began as an idea for summer racing in Florida. Stephen Calder, an area business and real estate developer, initially pushed to get the legislature to authorize summer racing in 1965. In 1966 dates for summer racing were put on the calendar at existing Tropical Park. Five years later on May 6, 1971, Calder Race Course officially opened.

PENNE WITH VODKA CREAM SAUCE

1 (29-ounce) can plum tomatoes
1 tablespoon butter
1 tablespoon olive oil
1 medium onion, chopped
1 cup heavy cream
¼ cup vodka
¼ teaspoon dried red pepper flakes
½ pound (8 ounces) penne pasta
¼ cup freshly grated Parmesan cheese
1 teaspoon minced fresh chives

Drain, seed, and chop the tomatoes. In a heavy-bottomed, large saucepan, sauté the onion in the butter and oil until the onion is translucent, about 10 minutes. Stir to keep the onion from sticking to the pan.

Boil water in a large saucepan over high heat. Add the penne pasta and cook according to package directions. Drain and toss to remove all water.

While the pasta is cooking, continue preparing the sauce. Add in the tomatoes and cook until almost no liquid remains in the pan, stirring frequently. Add in the cream, vodka, and pepper flakes. Cook until the sauce has the consistency you like. Serve immediately over the pasta with freshly grated Parmesan cheese and minced chives. Yield: 4 servings.

Full-card simulcasting was tried during Calder's twenty-fifth anniversary season in 1995 and expanded in 1997. It allows racing fans at one track to bet on races at other tracks around the country. At Arlington, for example, we once had the option of betting on eighty-one races! As simulcasting expanded at Calder, purses increased, and Calder revamped its

Champion Princess Rooney notched many of her early triumphs at Calder Race Course.

stakes schedule, attracting better horses.

Calder is home to the Princess Rooney Handicap, a graded race with a purse of $400,000. The race honors a great mare who began her career there. Princess Rooney is one of those racing legends that every horseman or horsewoman hopes to experience. Like Seattle Slew before her, Princess Rooney was purchased as a yearling for a moderate price. The owners named her for their daughter, whom they referred to as "princess" and whose middle name was Rooney.

Princess Rooney's first four races were at Calder, and she won all of them. She raced at ages two, three, and four and won seventeen races out of twenty-one starts, most of them

Calder opened in 1971 and is the summertime place to race in Florida.

graded stakes (many grade I), and earned a title as champion older mare of 1984. She failed to place only once. She raced against the best fillies and mares of her generation and once beat the boys. She retired at four, not due to injury or any reason other than, as one of her owners put it, "She's done everything; there's nothing left for her to prove."

The stakes race honoring her takes place around Bastille Day — July 14. If you're in

South Florida during that time, check the Calder race card and see who's running.

And while you're enjoying a day at the races, be sure and sample the food.

Calder's chef, Conroy Smith, prides himself on his use of local ingredients. With fresh broiled or grilled fish like tuna or swordfish steaks, he serves his **Mango-Papaya Salsa**. This is easy to make and can accompany any good grilled white fish. The combination is a perfect entrée for an outdoor summer dinner.

> ### MANGO-PAPAYA SALSA
>
> **1 ripe mango, peeled & chopped**
> **1 ripe papaya, peeled & chopped**
> **½ tablespoon chopped cilantro**
> **½ teaspoon diced jalapeño pepper**
> **½ tablespoon fresh lime juice**
> **Salt & freshly ground pepper to taste**
>
> ---
>
> In a small bowl, place the peeled and chopped fruit. Sprinkle the cilantro and diced jalapeño pepper over the fruit; then sprinkle the lime juice over all. Stir to blend and add the salt and freshly ground pepper to taste. Serve over or on the side of the fish as it comes off the grill. Yield: 4 servings.

The advent of farm-raised salmon has made this fish ubiquitous on restaurant menus. **Herb-Crusted Salmon Salad** is a dish for which the fish can be prepared ahead and served at room temperature, if desired. It's equally good hot.

When it comes to dessert, comfort food seems to be the heavy favorite at racetrack restaurants. After all, no matter how many horses compete in a race, only one usually wins. That leaves all those other owners, trainers, horseplayers, and fans in need of solace. Regardless of performance, all the horses get a bath, grooming, water, eventually food, and the comfort of their groom. The humans get dessert. At Calder they can order **Apricot-Coconut Bread Pudding.**

This recipe is fabulous. I tested it for a Sunday morning breakfast dish. No one noticed that it was supposed to be a dinner dessert, and it was consumed to the last coconut flake. When you're testing recipes for a cookbook, you have to be careful. If you make dishes like this one when you're not having company, you might end up eating the entire dish. Eating a whole pan of this would definitely put one on the path to outgrowing all one's clothes rapidly.

My sister reports that this dessert/brunch dish holds well as a leftover, too. She found a

FLORIDA

FLORIDA

HERB-CRUSTED SALMON SALAD

4 (6-ounce) fillets fresh salmon
Salt & freshly ground black pepper
4 tablespoons Dijon mustard

Herb mixture:
 1½ cups Japanese-style bread crumbs (panko)*
 ¼ cup freshly grated Parmesan cheese
 ¼ cup finely chopped fresh basil
 ¼ cup finely chopped fresh flat-leaf parsley
 2 tablespoons dried oregano
 2 tablespoons dried thyme
 1 tablespoon garlic powder
 2 – 4 tablespoons butter

Panko is available at gourmet food shops and Asian markets.

Sprinkle the salmon fillets with salt and pepper. Spread the mustard evenly on the top side of the fillets.

Combine the bread crumbs with the cheese, herbs, and garlic powder and mix well to blend completely. Put in a shallow bowl — a pasta bowl is perfect for this.

Preheat the oven to 425 degrees. Press the mustard-coated fillets into the crumb mixture and put on a platter.

Heat the butter in a large, heavy-bottomed sauté pan over medium-high heat. Put the coated salmon fillets in the pan. Cook for 2 – 3 minutes; then put the pan in the oven to finish cooking and brown the crumb topping, about 15 minutes. Watch the fish carefully because cooking time depends on the thickness of the fillets. Remove at once. These may be served hot or at room temperature. Chilling may make the breading soggy.

Serve on a bed of baby lettuces tossed with the raspberry vinaigrette. Yield: 4 servings.

leftover piece in her refrigerator some days after she had served it and said the pudding was neither soggy nor stale. "Just as good," she pronounced.

Calder Race Course, like many racetracks, has its own special cocktail. Called the **Calder Southern Comfort Hurricane**, the drink is easy to prepare, which is good because after the first one, you're going to need all the help you can get.

This concoction should console you for missing the Pick Six by one horse. Remember, close only counts in horseshoes, hand grenades, and dancing.

GULFSTREAM PARK

Gulfstream Park is Florida's flag-

RASPBERRY VINAIGRETTE

2 tablespoons raspberry vinegar
½ teaspoon honey
1 teaspoon finely minced garlic
1 teaspoon Dijon mustard
Salt & freshly ground black pepper
½ cup cold-pressed extra virgin olive oil

Combine the vinegar, honey, garlic, mustard, and salt and pepper; mix well. Slowly whisk in the olive oil until the vinaigrette is completely blended.

62

APRICOT-COCONUT BREAD PUDDING

1 baguette, cut into cubes	1 teaspoon vanilla extract
½ cup finely chopped sun-dried apricots	½ cup sugar, divided
1 cup whole milk	3 egg yolks
1 cup coconut milk*	1 cup shredded coconut**
½ (15-ounce) can coconut cream*	

Both coconut milk and coconut cream are available in supermarkets in the ethnic food section. Both Thai and Latino cuisines use these, so they are now available just about everywhere.

**Try to find unsweetened shredded coconut.*

Put the cubed bread in a well-buttered oven-proof 9x13x2" pan. Scatter the apricots over the bread. Preheat the oven to 350 degrees.

Heat the milk, coconut milk, coconut cream, vanilla extract, and half the sugar together. Stir and heat just to simmer, being sure the sugar melts and is fully incorporated. Remove from heat.

Beat the egg yolks with the remaining sugar until thick and lemon-colored. Slowly add the hot milk to the egg mixture, whisking constantly.

Pour the milk-egg mixture over the bread in the pan. Sprinkle the coconut and stir to blend everything together. Cover the pan with foil and put in the oven. After 45 minutes, remove the foil and return the pan to the oven so the top of the pudding can brown. May be served warm or room temperature. Yield: 6 servings.

ship racetrack and first opened in 1939. A four-day meet was held and that was it for the next few years. The track was closed because of World War II and reopened in 1944 for a brief meeting, then a full forty-day meeting in 1945.

Gulfstream hosts the Florida Derby, a middle-aged race, its fiftieth running contested in 2002. In 1952 Sky Ship, who had a modest racing and stallion career, won its inaugural running.

CALDER SOUTHERN COMFORT HURRICANE

1½ ounces Southern Comfort
½ ounce grenadine
Lemon-lime soda

In a tall glass filled with ice, pour the Southern Comfort and the grenadine. Fill with the lemon-lime soda and stir. Garnish with an orange slice and a cherry. Serve immediately. Serves one.

More notable winners of the Florida Derby have included Northern Dancer, Alydar, Spectacular Bid, Cryptoclearance, Unbridled, and Thunder Gulch. With the exception of Cryptoclearance and Alydar, the aforementioned also won the Kentucky Derby. The latest Florida Derby winner to take the Kentucky Derby was Monarchos in 2001. The Florida Derby, not surprisingly, is a good indicator of whom you might see in the starting gate the first Saturday in May.

A year after its inaugural running, the Florida Derby became the first stakes race in the state with a $100,000 purse, which in 1953 was a lot of money. In 2002 the Florida Derby carried a purse of one million dollars, which shows that horse racing purses have to keep up with inflation.

To have such a relatively short history, Gulfstream is rich in accomplishment. The track

Monarchos won the 2001 Florida Derby en route to victory in the Kentucky Derby.

Gulfstream Park opened in 1939 and is the home of the Florida Derby.

has hosted the Breeders' Cup championship races three times (1989, 1992, 1999), and in 1992 Julie Krone became the first female rider to win the riding title at Gulfstream with seventy-two wins.

Quality racing is not the only rich tradition at Gulfstream. The food at Gulfstream Park has been taken over by the team that runs Siro's, a well-known restaurant in Saratoga Springs, New York, another center of Thoroughbred racing.

Good food is as much a part, albeit smaller, of horse racing as the horses themselves. Since Florida is surrounded by salt water teeming with fish and shellfish, restaurants take

CRUSTY BAKED FLOUNDER
WITH CARAMELIZED BANANAS
& MANGO SALSA

4 flounder fillets, about 6 ounces each
2 cups unbleached flour
2 eggs, well beaten
½ cup heavy cream
2 – 3 cups panko (Japanese bread crumbs)
Olive oil for frying
Salt & freshly ground black pepper

Set up a breading station with the flour, the eggs beaten with the cream, and the panko or Japanese bread crumbs, each in a separate dish or bowl. Season the fillets with salt and pepper and completely coat them with the flour so there are no wet spots. Then completely coat the fillets with egg wash so there are no dry spots. Finally, dip the fillets in the panko, this time so there are no wet spots.

Preheat the oven to 350 degrees. Heat a large sauté pan over medium-high heat. Add enough oil to a depth of about ½ inch and turn the heat down to medium. Add the coated flounder fillets and cook until lightly browned, about 2 – 4 minutes. Turn the fillets over and place the pan in the oven and bake for 4 – 5 minutes. Remove the pan from the oven and drain the fish on paper towels. Serve immediately with a caramelized banana and the mango salsa. Yield: 4 servings.

CARAMELIZED
BANANAS

½ cup molasses
2 tablespoons dark rum
2 bananas

Combine the molasses and rum; mix well. Split the bananas lengthwise with the skin on. Brush the molasses mixture onto the banana flesh and place under a hot broiler and cook until the molasses bubbles and starts to brown. Serve immediately.

MANGO SALSA

1 cup mango, peeled, cut into ¼-inch dice
1 cup cantaloupe, cut into ¼-inch dice
½ medium red onion, finely diced
½ cup diced red bell pepper
3 green onions, sliced thin
½ small jalapeño, minced
3 sprigs cilantro, leaves chopped
Salt

Combine the fruits, vegetables, and leaves from the cilantro sprigs and season with salt. Let it sit overnight, covered, in the refrigerator. Allow the salsa to come to room temperature before serving.

Ocala is the center of Thoroughbred breeding in Florida.

advantage of this regional bounty. This Gulfstream Park recipe for **Crusty Baked Flounder with Caramelized Bananas & Mango Salsa** is both tropical and unusual.

Close to Gulfstream Park is Ft. Lauderdale. Burt & Jack's in Ft. Lauderdale is an after-the-races favorite. It is also the successful collaboration of restaurateur Jack Jackson and actor Burt Reynolds, a Florida native. The restaurant's **Baked Stuffed Maine Lobster** is a racing fan favorite.

This dish is so rich it is difficult to decide what to serve with it. The simpler, the better: a tossed green salad with a light vinaigrette and fresh fruit for dessert.

If you prefer a heartier dessert, try this dish from Burt & Jack's. I would bet good money that the restaurant is known for its **Bananas Wellington in Raspberry Sauce**. It's pretty

wonderful. If you're going to make it for friends, be sure to have everything organized and right at hand because it's one of those recipes that once begun move swiftly. It's a showy dessert, too, making a wonderful presentation.

You may have noticed a lot of bananas in the Florida chapter. They actually grow in the state, although not in the quantities that Central America produces.

Tastes of tropical paradise, a Kentucky Derby preview, and a fat-pursed stakes in tribute to a great race mare — what more could a good cook and horse enthusiast ask?

BAKED STUFFED MAINE LOBSTER

3 cups Ritz® cracker crumbs
8 sprigs flat-leaf parsley, chopped
⅛ teaspoon Spanish paprika
¼ teaspoon white pepper
1 stalk celery, chopped
4 (1¼ – 1½ pound) Maine lobsters
½ cup melted butter
½ small onion, chopped

½ red or green bell pepper, chopped
2 cloves garlic, minced
½ cup (4 ounces) dry sherry
1 tablespoon Worcestershire sauce
4 tablespoons melted butter
½ cup freshly grated Parmesan cheese
Lemon wedges
¾ cup melted butter

To make the stuffing, pulverize the Ritz® crackers and put them in a medium mixing bowl. You can put them in a plastic bag and pulverize with a rolling pin or put them in a food processor and pulse till you have rough crumbs. Add in the parsley, paprika, and white pepper; toss to mix well.

In a heavy-bottomed saucepan melt the butter and add the onion, bell pepper, and garlic; cook over medium-low heat until the vegetables are tender and the onions translucent, about 10 minutes. Remove from the heat and add in the dry sherry and Worcestershire sauce; stir to incorporate.

Add the cracker mix to the vegetables and stir to mix well. Set aside and prepare the lobsters.

To cook the lobsters, place them in a large kettle in about 1½ inches of water on medium heat. Bring the water to a boil and watch carefully. As soon as the large claw turns red, remove the lobsters from the water and run under cold water to halt the cooking.

Turn on the broiler in the oven. Using poultry shears, remove the large claws and the knuckles from the body. Using a large chef's knife with a wide blade, split the lobster body lengthwise using one cleaver-like motion. Be sure to leave the shell intact. Using crackers and the poultry shears, remove the meat from the claws and knuckles and place the meat in the split lobster. Top with ½ cup of the stuffing, drip some melted butter over that, sprinkle with some of the freshly grated Parmesan, and put in the oven for 2 – 3 minutes to finish. Serve with lemon wedges and "drawn" butter. Yield: 4 servings.

BANANAS WELLINGTON IN RASPBERRY SAUCE

For the sauce:
1 pint raspberries
2 tablespoons sugar
1 tablespoon fresh lemon juice
1 teaspoon cornstarch

For the Wellington:
2 large, firm, ripe bananas*
8 sheets phyllo dough
8 ounces white chocolate
4 ounces toasted sliced almonds

Safflower or canola oil for frying
Confectioners' sugar for dusting

The banana skin should be completely yellow, with no green showing, but before the little brown freckles appear. The freckles indicate a completely ripe fruit and the banana may then be too soft for this recipe.

To prepare the sauce, put all the ingredients in a food processor and blend until smooth. Put the mixture in a saucepan and cook over medium heat, stirring occasionally, until the cornstarch thickens the sauce a little. Remove from the heat and reserve. May be made a day ahead and held in the refrigerator. Bring to room temperature before serving.

For the Wellington, thaw the phyllo dough in the refrigerator according to package directions. On a clean, clear work surface, place the sheets of dough. Peel the bananas, cut them in half lengthwise and then in half crosswise so you have four pieces from each banana. Place a piece of banana near the end of the sheet of phyllo dough closest to you. Sprinkle with a few pieces of white chocolate and some almonds. Using a pastry brush, wet the dough beside the piece of banana and fold over so the banana is covered. Fold both sides of the dough over the banana and roll the dough until you reach the end of sheet. Dampen with water brushed on and seal the ends and sides. Repeat with all the pieces of banana until you have 8 neat little packages ready to go.

Put several inches of the oil in a deep-sided saucepan and heat until a bread cube dropped in the fat sizzles and turns brown immediately. Drop the banana packages gently into the oil; cook about a minute and a half; turn and cook another minute and a half. If you can fit two or three at a time, do so. When the bananas are browned on both sides, remove with a slotted spoon onto paper towels. As soon as all the Bananas Wellington are cooked, plate them and serve.

On each plate place some of the raspberry sauce. Put a banana on the sauce; dust with confectioners' sugar and serve. Yield: 8 servings.

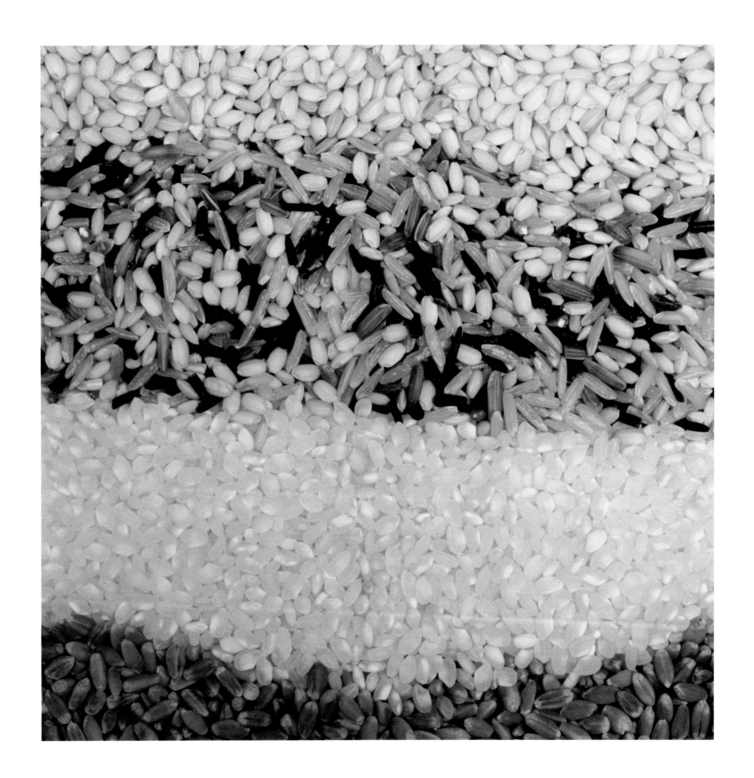

CHAPTER

4

KENTUCKY

KENTUCKY

KEENELAND & CHURCHILL DOWNS

Kentucky stretches from the Appalachian Mountains in the east all the way west to the Mississippi River. Between is some of the richest farmland in the country. Underlying the soil is a limestone shield that imparts to the grass both a slightly bluish tinge and a high calcium content ideal for the growth of strong bones in young Thoroughbred horses. This area was a natural to become the place to breed racehorses.

The Kentucky Bluegrass region is the epicenter of today's Thoroughbred breeding and racing industry. One visit to the September yearling sales at Keeneland will confirm this. More than three thousand young Thoroughbreds go through the auction ring over ten days in the largest sale of its kind anywhere in the world. These youngsters range from the most regally bred to the most modest. Among them are future winners of the Kentucky Derby, the Breeders' Cup Classic, and every other major race here and abroad. Along the shed rows, all the prominent trainers you see interviewed endlessly before the Derby and most of the prominent owners inspect yearlings from every angle and pencil cryptic notes on catalogue pages. Optimism is in the air.

Anyone who is serious about Thoroughbred racing and breeding has staked a claim in the Bluegrass. In addition to sixth-generation Kentuckians, international tycoons and Arab princes own Kentucky property and horses. All are intent on being major players, and Lexington is where they buy the horseflesh, strike the deals, and dream of glory. A few years ago a novice to the breeding part of the game fell in love with a broodmare and bought her for $13,000. He bred her to the young stallion Maria's Mon for another $7,500, and the resulting colt was none other than Monarchos, who won the Kentucky Derby in 2001 in near-record time. Lightning can strike at every part of this great sport.

In addition to sales, Keeneland conducts top-class racing. Keeneland has even enjoyed a

Graduates of the Keeneland sales win the world's major races and annually command prices of a million dollars and more.

private visit from England's Queen Elizabeth II, a noted horse racing enthusiast and owner. Three-week spring and fall meets lead up to some of the great, more well-known races elsewhere but provide plenty of excitement of their own. The spring meet dovetails into the Kentucky Derby and the Triple Crown. Keeneland's signature spring races for three-year-old colts, the Blue Grass and Lexington stakes, serve as major prep races for horses on the Triple Crown trail. Horses like Unbridled, Thunder Gulch, and Charismatic raced here before heading to Louisville and Churchill Downs.

When asked by a local publication what makes Keeneland special, one trainer commented that horses are a product of their environment and Keeneland's environment is perfect for young horses. Another said it's the high degree of maintenance and a very consistent racetrack.

In the fall the horses return to Keeneland to race in the rich line-up of stakes and to prepare for the Breeders' Cup, now billed as the World Thoroughbred Championships. The

Keeneland Race Course hosts the country's best-dressed and most knowledgeable racing fans.

The Spinster Stakes at Keeneland attracts the country's best fillies and mares.

Breeders' Cup moves each year to a different racing venue, and its eight races help determine divisional championships. Participants come from Europe, Japan, and the United Arab Emirates to compete. Keeneland's most prestigious fall race is the Spinster Stakes for fillies and mares. First run in 1956 and won that year by the great race mare Doubledogdare, the race is a good prep for the Breeders' Cup Distaff.

The cosmopolitan mix of participants in the horse industry has added culinary sophistication to the Bluegrass region and Louisville, home of Churchill Downs and the Kentucky Derby. Chefs at Keeneland, Churchill Downs, and surrounding eating establishments have successfully managed to infuse modern elements into Kentucky down-home recipes that

date back as far as Daniel Boone.

Other dishes with shorter histories, but just as much flavor, have been created or imported in recent years to cater to more sophisticated palates and have become house favorites.

Keeneland's food concessionaire, Turf Catering, puts this **Chicken & Toasted Almond Soup** on the menu to warm you if the weather's uncooperative and to comfort you if your horse has an off day. Or just to add to your feeling of general well being. This soup is much

---

CHICKEN & TOASTED ALMOND SOUP

1½ quarts chicken stock, homemade or canned	**Bay leaf**
1 large chicken breast, split	**½ cup white wine**
Small onion stuck with cloves	

Put the chicken stock, chicken breast, onion, bay leaf, and the wine in a large stockpot. Bring to a simmer and cook until the chicken breast is tender. Remove the chicken to a platter and cool. When the chicken is cool, remove the bones and skin. Cut into bite-sized pieces. Remove the onion and bay leaf and strain the broth. Put the broth back in the pan; keep warm.

¼ cup butter	**Diced, cooked chicken breast**
1 cup diced onion	**1¼ cups heavy cream, room temperature**
1 cup diced celery	**Salt & freshly ground pepper to taste**
3 – 4 tablespoons flour	**½ cup sliced, toasted almonds***
Reserved, warm chicken broth	**¼ cup finely chopped flat-leaf parsley**

To toast the sliced almonds, spread out in a brownie pan and put in a 325-degree oven until the almonds smell "toasty" and are slightly browned. Remove and reserve. DON'T EAT, no matter how good they smell and taste. They're for the soup!

In another heavy-bottomed saucepan, melt the butter and add the onions and celery. Cook over moderate heat, stirring to keep from sticking, until the onions are translucent and aromatic, about 10 minutes. Add the flour, stir in to blend, and make a roux. Cook for a few minutes to be sure the flour is blended well. Gradually add some of the warm chicken stock to the mixture, stirring to blend and avoid lumping. Once the mixture is smooth, add the rest of the broth and bring the soup just to the boil.

Remove from the heat. Add in the diced, cooked chicken breast, most of the almonds, and the parsley; then stir in the heavy cream to blend smoothly. Season to taste with salt and pepper. Ladle out into warmed soup bowls. Garnish with the remaining almonds and the parsley. Yield: 4 – 6 servings.

Doubledogdare won the inaugural Spinster Stakes and now has a race named in her honor.

better if you use a homemade or other rich chicken stock. The richer the stock, the deeper and more intense the flavor of this, or any soup, will be.

Another soup, one with a provenance that is southern France rather than the American South, is this dish from Dudley's, an after-the-races, after-the-sales favorite spot in Lexington. The recipe is for **Mussels Bourride**, a "blond" soup from Provence that involves aioli, that region's signature garlicky mayonnaise, fresh fish, sometimes a bit of crème fraiche, potatoes, fennel, leeks, and garlic. The bourride from Dudley's is a simpler dish, but delicious, nonetheless.

Spoonbread, a variation of corn bread, is definitely a speciality of the American South.

MUSSELS BOURRIDE

Make the aioli ahead of time and reserve. It will keep for two days in the refrigerator.

For the aioli:
4 good-sized cloves of garlic
¼ teaspoon Kosher salt

2 egg yolks
1 teaspoon fresh lemon juice
1 cup extra virgin olive oil

If you don't have a mortar and pestle, peel the garlic cloves and in a small mixing bowl, using the back of a wooden spoon, mash well. Add the salt and using the back of the spoon or the pestle, mash the salt into the garlic until combined into a smooth paste. Add the egg yolks, one at a time, and beat with a whisk or electric mixer until combined. Add in a little of the oil and whisk or beat again. With the beater running, add the rest of the oil in a thin, steady stream. The aioli will gradually thicken into a rich, redolent mayonnaise. Cover and refrigerate.

For the mussels, per person:
12 mussels, cleaned, beard removed
½ large shallot, julienned

½ cup good dry white wine
2 tablespoons aioli

Remove the aioli from the refrigerator; allow to come to room temperature. Place serving bowls in a warm oven with door open (175 degrees).

In a large sauté pan, sweat the shallots in the white wine over medium heat. Once the wine is simmering, add the mussels and cover the pan. Cook for 3 minutes, no more.

Mussels will open. Discard any that have not opened; they are bad.

Put the mussels in a heated bowl(s) and reserve the liquid in the pan.

Put the aioli in a bowl; whisk in the broth from the pan. Pour over the mussels and serve. A good, crusty loaf of bread needs to accompany this dish, for mopping up if nothing else. Yield: Enough aioli to serve 6.

The best I ever tasted was at the Boone Tavern in Berea, Kentucky. In fact, Berea holds a spoonbread festival every year. Here's a version of **Spoonbread** that seems to come close. Spoonbread does not keep and must be served right from the pan after leaving the oven.

Burgoo is a Kentucky dish that goes back far enough to have been made originally with game, especially squirrel. The early recipes called for various game meats, but all seemed to require squirrel. A book called *Cooking American*, compiled by Sidney Dean and filled with lore and recipes of regional American cooking, has this to say about burgoo:

"What the clambake is to the native Rhode Islander, the barbecue stew, or burgoo is to

SPOONBREAD

1 cup cornmeal	1 teaspoon salt
1 cup boiling water	2 teaspoons baking powder
1½ cups whole milk	3 eggs, well beaten
½ cup half & half cream	2 tablespoons melted butter

Liberally butter a deep 10-inch cast-iron skillet if you have one. Otherwise, butter an oven-proof baking dish, 9x12x2" or a round 2-quart casserole. Preheat the oven to 375 degrees.

Put the cornmeal in a bowl; pour the boiling water over it in a steady stream, stirring constantly to avoid lumping. Allow the cornmeal to cool slightly. Add the milk and cream to the cornmeal slowly, mixing in the salt and baking powder at the same time. Add the well-beaten eggs, and last, the melted butter. Pour into the pan and put in the oven. Bake for 30 – 40 minutes. The top should be golden; a knife or cake tester inserted in the center should come out clean. Serve immediately. Yield: 4 servings.

The horse and the sport of racing are celebrated in all their glory at Keeneland.

the native Kentuckian. Both of these magnificent meals typify American cooking in the most literal and historic sense of the words." The author reports that burgoo dates back at least to Daniel Boone and probably earlier. Dean provides a cut-down recipe of J.T. Looney's. During the 1930s and 1940s in Lexington, Looney was known as the burgoo king. Dean also cites a definition of the concoction I read in two other places, none giving a source, but it's pretty interesting folklore, so here it is:

"Burgoo is literally a soup composed of many vegetables and meats delectably fused together in an enormous caldron (sic), over which, at the exact moment, a rabbit's foot at the end of a yarn string is properly waved by a colored preacher, whose salary has been paid to date. These are the good omens by which burgoo is fortified."

Another definition given by the *New York Tribune* of 1891: [Burgoo is] "a sort of broth prepared from meat and vegetables and strongly seasoned with pepper and Kentucky whiskey."

The cooks at Turf Catering prepare giant vats of burgoo for Keeneland racing fans.

BURGOO

2 lamb shanks
1 pound stew beef, cut in cubes*
1 chicken (about 2½ pounds), cut up
3 – 4 tablespoons canola oil
2 quarts of water
½ teaspoon salt
1 cup chopped onion
2 tablespoons Worcestershire sauce
1 large garlic clove, chopped
1 can (1 pound, 3 ounces) chopped tomatoes
1 (10-ounce) package frozen butter beans,
   limas may be substituted

3 carrots, diced
½ cup chopped flat-leaf parsley
2 cups diced potatoes (Yukon Gold, Finn,
   or other boiling potato)
1 small onion, stuck with 12 cloves
3 stalks celery, with leaves, chopped fine
2 bay leaves
1 (10-ounce) package frozen okra
1 (10-ounce) package frozen corn,
   or 2 ears fresh, cut off the cob
½ cup red wine
¼ teaspoon red pepper flakes

Optional — use ½ beef and ½ pork, cut in cubes.

In a heavy-bottomed stewing kettle, preferably cast-iron, over medium heat, brown the lamb shanks and the beef (and pork) in 2 – 3 tablespoons of the oil. You may have to brown the meat in batches. When the meat is browned, remove to a platter and brown the chicken. Put the other meats back in the kettle and add the water.

In another saucepan, cook the onions in the remaining oil until they are translucent, about 10 minutes. Add the Worcestershire sauce. Add the onions, salt, and chopped garlic clove to the meat and simmer, covered, over low heat until the meat is tender and falling off the bones, about 1½ – 2 hours. (The pot should be just barely simmering.) Remove the meat to a platter and when cool enough to handle, remove skin, bones, and any cartilage. Cut the meat in large chunks as it comes off the bones. Return the meat to the kettle.

Add the tomatoes, carrots, butter beans, parsley, potatoes, celery, and onion stuck with cloves. Add the bay leaves and cover the pot and return to a low simmer. Cook until everything is tender and well blended. Stir occasionally to be sure the burgoo is not sticking to the bottom of the pan. Once cooked, the burgoo should sit overnight for fullest flavor.

Fifteen minutes before you are ready to serve, remove the onion stuck with cloves and the bay leaves, if you can find them. Add the corn, okra, and the red wine and continue cooking. Yield: 8 – 10 servings.

KENTUCKY

ROBERT'S RAJUN CAJUN "BEGINNER'S LUCK" CHILI

4 tablespoons olive oil
1 cup chopped onions
2 pounds lean ground beef
1 pound spicy sausage
2½ tablespoons dark chili powder
1 tablespoon paprika
Salt to taste
1 tablespoon ground cumin
1 tablespoon Tabasco® or other hot sauce
1 tablespoon powdered garlic
2 tablespoons Worcestershire sauce
1 (14½-ounce) can diced tomatoes
2 (14½-ounce) cans chili beans
3½ cups tomato juice
1 (12-ounce) bottle beer (optional)

In a large cast-iron skillet, over medium heat, put the olive oil and the onions. Cook the onions until translucent, about 10 minutes. Add the hamburger and sausage, crumbling the meat as you add it in. Stir occasionally as the meat browns to keep it from sticking. Sprinkle the meat with the chili powder, paprika, cumin, hot sauce, garlic powder, and last of all, the Worcestershire sauce. After each addition stir the mixture to blend the spices into the meat.

In a large, heavy-bottomed soup kettle, put the tomatoes, chili beans, and tomato juice. When all the meat is browned, add it to the tomato mixture and simmer over low heat for an hour and a half to blend all the flavors. Stir often to be sure nothing's sticking to the pan. If the chili thickens too much, add more tomato juice. Cool, cover, and refrigerate overnight. Reheat before serving. Yield: 2 – 3 quarts of chili.

Even without the whiskey, burgoo is a specifically Kentucky dish. There are those folks living in Illinois border towns who might argue, but they're only laying claim to something that's really not theirs.

Burgoo as it's known in Kentucky is a rich stew of several meats, anything the garden might yield, and some seasoning, cooked until it's an amalgam that sticks to the ribs and comforts the bereft. It was once used to get people elected to office. Naturally it's on the menu at Keeneland and naturally Turf Catering's Mike Wolken, the executive chef, won't part with his recipe. He says it's the one that originated with Looney, who even had a horse named after him to honor his culinary tradition. The four-legged Burgoo King won the Kentucky Derby in 1932. He was also the first winner to wear the "blanket of roses."

After wheedling some information out of Mike about red wine and possible spicing and after reading more burgoo recipes than I care to count — some say there are as many as 150,000 recipes for this dish — I came up with this version of **Burgoo**, which I think is pretty close to the dish served at Keeneland.

With burgoo, you need only a good green salad with a pleasant vinaigrette dressing, a crusty loaf or some corn bread, and the rest of the red wine for a great winter meal.

The Blood-Horse is the flagship publication of the Thoroughbred Owners and Breeders Association. As such, it has the responsibility of putting out a weekly magazine with all the latest racing news, breathtaking photos, and up-to-date breeding information. Besides all that, its employees also indulge in frequent potlucks. Here's one of the company's more renowned dishes, **Robert's Rajun Cajun "Beginner's Luck" Chili**, contributed by Robert Bolson, the corporate marketing manager.

My fifteen-year-old niece says this is the best chili ever. Period.

This **Corn Bread Salad** from Keeneland is one that could stand alone on a hot summer evening or be part of a larger meal and a pretty, as well as interesting, addition to a buffet table or tailgate party. It might also make a great accompaniment to the raging chili above. It is an interesting variation on both salad and corn bread. Bread salad is a traditional Italian dish and delicious if made well. This is a southern riff on that dish.

In our grandparents' day, chicken was a luxury often reserved for Sunday dinner after church. Now it's ubiquitous, appearing everywhere and in forms scarcely dreamed of a few years ago. Who knew that chickens had fingers, for instance? Hiding under all those feathers, one supposes. Keeneland's dining rooms give chicken the old-fashioned luxury treatment in this **Chicken Français**.

What is life without dessert? There are those who feel you should eat dessert first, as life is uncertain. Here's one you can eat before or after, depending on your faith in the next thirty minutes. Called **Warm Chocolate Bliss**, it's Dudley's gift to chocoholics everywhere

CORN BREAD SALAD

- 1 pan corn bread (9x12x2")*
- 1 cup seeded, diced tomatoes
- 1 cup diced red bell pepper
- 1 cup diced yellow bell pepper
- ½ cup diced green onions
- 1 cup sweet pickle relish, drained
- 1 cup crisp, cooked bacon, broken into small pieces
- 2 cups mayonnaise

* The corn bread should be savory, that is have no sugar in it. You will need a double batch or 2 boxes of corn bread mix, which also works.

Crumble or cut the cooled corn bread into bite-sized pieces.

Put the tomatoes, peppers, and onions in a large bowl and toss to mix well.

Put the drained pickle relish in a bowl; add the bacon bits and mayonnaise and mix well.

In a large glass bowl, layer the corn bread, vegetables, and the dressing. Cover with plastic wrap and return to the refrigerator and keep several hours or overnight to allow flavors to blend. Yield: 8 – 10 servings.

and incorporates another Kentucky product: bourbon. This is one of the best chocolate desserts I have ever eaten and, trust me, I have been a serious, dedicated chocolate eater all my life.

The distance from Lexington to Louisville is a short seventy to eighty miles. The road is much longer if you're a Thoroughbred of whom great things are expected — three years of hopes and dreams and time and money and lots of frequent flyer miles commuting to prep races. In between, your owner(s), trainer, exercise rider(s), groom, and all the other humans who have a vested interest in your welfare alternate among hope, despair, and wild euphoria as you win one or two important prep races, don't even place in others, and generally behave like the very young racehorse you are.

CHICKEN FRANÇAIS

Marinade:
- ½ cup olive oil
- ½ cup red wine vinegar
- 1½ teaspoons Worcestershire sauce
- ½ teaspoon Tabasco® sauce
- Freshly ground black pepper
- ¼ cup soy sauce
- 1½ teaspoons chopped fresh garlic
- ¼ cup chopped flat-leaf parsley
- ¼ cup chopped green onion

Pinch (⅛ teaspoon) cayenne

Chicken:
- 4 boneless chicken breasts (6 – 8 ounce), skin removed
- 1 cup flour
- 3 eggs, well beaten
- ½ cup freshly grated Parmesan cheese
- 2 teaspoons chopped flat-leaf parsley
- ½ cup safflower oil or butter, or combination of two
- 1 cup marinade

For the marinade, whip the oil and vinegar together. Add the other marinade ingredients and blend well. Check for taste. Add more garlic if desired. Marinade may be held at room temperature for 3 days.

Pound the chicken breasts till even and flat; they should be about ½-inch thick. Beat the eggs with the cheese and parsley. Put the flour in a shallow bowl and dredge the chicken breasts until completely coated with no wet spots. Then dip them into the beaten egg mixture until the chicken is completely coated.

Have the butter/oil hot and fry the chicken breasts quickly until both sides are golden brown. (Dish can be made one day in advance to this point.) Preheat the oven to 350 degrees. Put the chicken breasts in a shallow oven-proof dish and drizzle the marinade over them. Put the pan in the oven and bake for approximately 15 minutes. Pour additional marinade over the chicken after serving, or pass the marinade in a warmed sauceboat. Serve with wild rice or garlic mashed potatoes. Yield: 4 servings.

The hope is you'll make it to the Kentucky Derby, which was modeled on the Epsom Derby in England. It takes place the first Saturday in May at Churchill Downs and is the first race of the Triple Crown, one of the most difficult goals in all of sports to achieve. The three races take place over five weeks, a trying task that requires tremendous physical effort by these young horses. It is comparable to asking a tennis player to win three of four Grand Slam tournaments in five weeks instead of five months.

Only eleven horses that have won the Derby have gone on to win the Triple Crown, a pretty small and intimidating number. Amazingly, three of those Triple Crown victories occurred during the 1970s: Secretariat, Seattle Slew, and Affirmed. Not since Affirmed's sweep in 1978 has a horse won all three, although several have come close, winning two of the three races.

WARM CHOCOLATE BLISS

¼ **cup Kentucky bourbon**
⅔ **cup sugar**
⅔ **cup bittersweet chocolate chips***
½ **cup melted unsalted butter**
3 eggs, well beaten, room temperature

* If you use the mini-chips, they will melt faster.

Preheat the oven to 350 degrees. Generously butter a small (6-inch) soufflé dish or two ramekins; set aside. Put the teakettle or a pan of water on to warm.

Put the chocolate chips in a mixing bowl. Mix the bourbon and the sugar together in a small, heavy-bottomed saucepan. Bring to a boil over medium heat; stir to dissolve the sugar. Remove from the heat and pour over the chocolate chips. Stir until the chocolate is melted and the mixture is completely blended.

Add the melted butter; blend in. Add the eggs and whisk briskly to incorporate fully. Pour into the buttered small soufflé dish or two ramekins. Cover it/them with foil and put in a larger, oven-proof pan. Pour the hot water into the pan, filling about three-quarters of the way up. Bake the bliss for 30 minutes for the single dish, 20 – 25 for the two smaller dishes.

Remove from the water bath, remove the foil, and allow to cool for 5 minutes. Invert on service plate and top with ice cream; dust with cinnamon or cocoa powder to serve. Note: The center of the bliss should be molten. Yield: 2 servings.

LOUISVILLE, THE TWIN SPIRES, AND THE DERBY

Racing in Louisville began as early as 1783 and continued at a variety of places until the Oakland Race Course opened in 1833. In 1858 the Woodlawn course, just east of Louisville, replaced Oakland. After only twelve years of operation it, too, closed. The Woodlawn Vase, the track's most important trophy, through a very circuitous route became the cup presented to the winner of the Preakness Stakes in 1917. It remains the oldest and most valuable trophy in American racing.

KENTUCKY

In 1874 Colonel M. Lewis Clark, having toured England and France, returned with the idea of establishing a Kentucky Jockey Club to conduct race meets. He enlisted the aid of other prominent Louisvillians, and the Kentucky Jockey Club was incorporated on June 20 of that year. Clark then sold memberships at one hundred dollars apiece and raised $32,000. He used the money to lease eighty acres from his uncles John and Henry Churchill and built the track, grandstand, clubhouse, and stables. For the initial meet in 1875, Clark conceived the Kentucky Derby and the Kentucky Oaks, modeled, respectively, on the Epsom Derby and the Epsom Oaks. That was the beginning of America's most fabled race and the track at which it is run each year.

In 1894 William Schulte took over as president and a new grandstand was built. The twin spires were the design of Joseph P. Baldez, a twenty-four-year-old architectural draftsman. No one foresaw that his twin spires would become known worldwide. The grandstand was finished just in time for the running of the twenty-first Derby, won by Halma, who further distinguished himself by siring the winner of the twenty-eighth Derby, Alan-a-Dale.

Much has changed about Churchill Downs over the years, yet the Kentucky Derby and the twin spires remain permanent fixtures.

In 1923 in downtown Louisville, an elegant hotel was built on Fourth Street and quickly became the place to stay on Derby weekend. Some famous names graced the Brown Hotel's guest register right from the start: Walter Huston, Irene Dunne, Bing Crosby, Sam Snead, Mr. and Mrs. Walt Disney, and the Duke of Windsor among many, many others.

It was also a place where you went to eat and eat well. One of the legendary dishes to come out of the Brown Hotel's kitchens was an open-faced sandwich called "The Hot Brown," the creation of head chef Fred K. Schmidt. Those who grew up in Louisville during this time say the **Original Hot Brown** has never been matched. Here, we give both the original Hot Brown recipe and one updated for modern palates and with additions made over time.

The updated Hot Brown now includes tomato slices. I was unable to discover who made this addition or when it first appeared on restaurant menus around Kentucky. But it is a worthwhile addi-

The famed blanket of roses bedecks each year's Derby winner.

tion, adding both taste and texture to the Hot Brown.

The **Modern Hot Brown** requires good-quality white bread. Supermarket bread, what the French call *pain industriel* will dissolve back to dough under the hot cheese sauce. Also, purchase good-quality cheese and grate it fresh. The stuff that comes in those green foil cardboard containers has more to do with sawdust than it does with food. You don't have to wait for Thanksgiving to try this one out; most good deli counters now have real roast turkey breast for sale. Don't use that rolled turkey that looks like lunchmeat — what the French might call *dindon industriel*.

Churchill Downs has a new food service crew headed by executive chef Ron Krivosik. He's also the exec in charge of the food at Arlington. So you can dine well in two places not all that far apart and enjoy the races at both. **Roasted Lemon-Garlic Chicken Breasts**

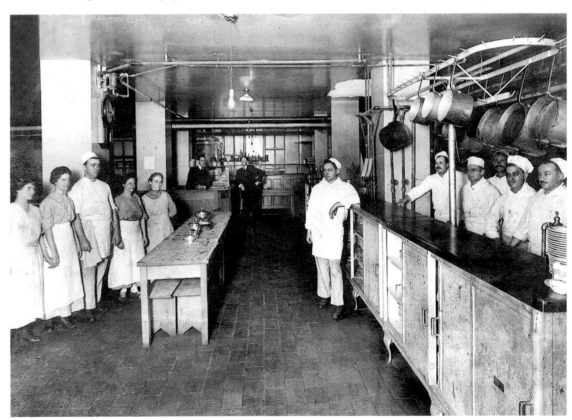

Fred K. Schmidt, shown with staff in the kitchen of the Brown Hotel, created the Hot Brown.

ORIGINAL HOT BROWN

4 ounces butter
6 tablespoons flour
3 – 3½ cups milk
1 beaten egg
6 tablespoons freshly grated Parmesan cheese
1 ounce whipped cream, optional

Salt & pepper to taste
Slices of roasted turkey
8 – 12 slices of toast, trimmed
Extra grated Parmesan cheese
8 – 12 strips crisp, cooked bacon

Melt butter and add enough of the flour to make a reasonably thick roux (enough to absorb all the butter). Add the milk and Parmesan cheese. Add the well-beaten egg to thicken the sauce, but do not allow it to boil. Remove from the heat. Fold in the whipped cream, if desired. Add salt and pepper to taste.

For each Hot Brown, place two slices of toast in a metal or flame-proof dish. Cover the toast with slices of roasted turkey. Pour a generous amount of the sauce over the turkey and toast. Sprinkle with some of the additional Parmesan cheese. Place the dish under the broiler until the sauce is speckled on top and bubbly. Remove from the broiler; place two pieces of the bacon, crossed, on top and serve immediately. Yield: 4 – 6 servings.

MODERN HOT BROWN

2 tablespoons unsalted butter
3 tablespoons unbleached flour
1½ cups milk, scalded
2 ounces amber beer
3 ounces Gruyere cheese, grated

4 slices good white bread, toasted lightly
½ pound sliced roasted turkey breast
4 thin slices ripe tomato
8 slices crisp, cooked bacon
3 – 4 tablespoons freshly grated Parmesan cheese

In a small, heavy-bottomed saucepan, scald the milk; set aside. That is, bring the milk just to the boiling point and remove from the heat. Toast the bread. Set aside. Cook the bacon, drain on paper towels, and set aside.

In a heavy-bottomed saucepan, melt the butter over medium heat. Stir in the flour and whisk briskly to make the roux and cook the flour a little. (This eliminates the floury taste.) Add the milk in a steady stream, whisking well to incorporate. Remove from the heat. Add in the grated Gruyere and continue whisking until the cheese is melted and sauce is smooth. Add in the beer and season to taste with salt and pepper.

Arrange the toast slices in an oven-proof dish, place the sliced turkey on top of the toast, and then place the sliced tomatoes on top of the turkey. Top with the sauce, sprinkle with the freshly grated Parmesan cheese, and place under the broiler until "speckled brown and bubbly." Remove from the broiler, place the crossed pieces of bacon on top, and serve immediately. Yield: 4 servings.

ROASTED LEMON-GARLIC CHICKEN BREASTS WITH LEMON SAUCE

8 chicken breasts (8 – 10 ounce), skin on, bone in
(or 4 whole breasts, split)
12 – 14 lemons, depending on size

For the marinade:
1 cup fresh-squeezed lemon juice
2 ounces corn oil
½ cup chopped fresh rosemary
1 tablespoon dried oregano
1 teaspoon dried red pepper flakes
2 tablespoons minced fresh garlic
Kosher salt to taste

Freshly ground black pepper to taste

For the sauce:
½ cup fresh-squeezed lemon juice
¼ cup extra virgin olive oil
½ teaspoon minced fresh garlic
¼ teaspoon dried oregano
¼ teaspoon red wine vinegar
½ cup veal demi-glace (reduced veal stock)*

Kosher salt to taste
Freshly ground black pepper to taste

Demi-glace is a rich brown sauce that combines veal (or beef) stock with madeira or sherry. It is slowly cooked until reduced by half to a thick glaze that coats a spoon.

Clean and trim the chicken breasts. Prepare the marinade by combining the lemon juice, corn oil, rosemary, oregano, red pepper flakes, and garlic in a deep bowl. Whisk to blend well. (The bowl needs to be big enough to hold the marinade and all the chicken breasts.)

Season the chicken breasts with the salt and pepper and place in the bowl with the marinade. Coat each chicken breast thoroughly with the marinade. Cover the bowl and marinate the chicken breasts overnight in the refrigerator.

Preheat the oven to 400 degrees. Place the marinated chicken in a deep-sided baking dish, skin side up, in a single layer. Put the dish in the preheated oven and roast the chicken for 30 – 40 minutes or until 95% cooked.

While the chicken is cooking, make the sauce. Whisk the lemon juice, olive oil, garlic, and red wine vinegar together in a medium saucepan. Bring to a boil over high heat; then turn heat off. Add the veal glace and whisk to incorporate. Check for seasoning; add salt and pepper if necessary.

Pour the lemon sauce over the nearly cooked chicken, turn the oven up to 450 degrees, and finish roasting the chicken until it is a golden brown and the skin is very crisp, about 10 minutes.

Remove the chicken from the oven and let rest in the pan about 20 minutes, lightly covered with a sheet of aluminum foil. Put the chicken breasts on a serving platter or individual plates, spoon some of the sauce over them, and enjoy!
Yield: 8 servings.

with Lemon Sauce involves lots of lemon and lots of garlic and has been pronounced very delicious by our testers. A good dish for company as you can make it ahead.

Another way of serving chicken, one that works with a small group or a very large one, is chicken salad. Good chicken salad requires the best ingredients and attention to the details. The reward is a dish that others will beg you for the recipe so they can make it at home.

Good chicken salad is handy for entertaining and tailgating during Derby weekend and other important horse-related events such as the September yearling sale at Keeneland, various national and international competitions at the Kentucky Horse Park, and, of course, the race meetings held at Keeneland, Churchill Downs, and the other Kentucky tracks.

You should enjoy making and eating this **Chicken Salad**, which is one served often in Kentucky. It can be served as a salad, properly garnished with red and yellow bell peppers, hard-boiled egg, or whatever appeals to your culinary and artistic instincts. It can also be put on good bread and made into small finger sandwiches for a buffet. For the finger sandwiches, the meat and other components should be chopped fine.

CHICKEN SALAD

1 chicken, cut up
1 cup good white wine
5 cups water, enough to cover chicken
1 medium onion, peeled
Bay leaf
12 whole peppercorns
1 cup chopped celery, leaves included
1 cup chopped mild onion
¾ cup chopped, toasted pecans
1 cup good mayonnaise*

* Use a mayonnaise that consists of egg, oil, lemon juice and/or vinegar and nothing else. Homemade is best, of course.

Put the chicken, wine, water, whole onion, bay leaf, and peppercorns in a large kettle. Place over low heat and bring to a simmer. Keep at a bare simmer until the chicken tests done by inserting a fork into the meatiest parts, about 20 – 30 minutes. Remove the chicken from the pot onto a platter and allow it to come to room temperature.

Strain and reserve the broth. You can de-fat it, then freeze for later use.

Remove all the skin, bones, and cartilage from the chicken. Discard those and cut the chicken into bite-sized pieces.

Preheat the oven to 275 degrees. Toast the pecans by spreading them out in a brownie pan and placing in the preheated oven. When the pecans start to smell toasty and are slightly browned, they're done. Remove and cool to room temperature.

Put the chicken in a large bowl. Add the celery, chopped onion, and pecans and toss to mix well. Then add the mayonnaise, stirring to blend it all together. Cover and refrigerate. The salad can be made a day ahead and is actually better if you can manage it. Yield: 6 main servings or 12 sandwiches, cut up.

CHEESE GRITS CASSEROLE

3 cups water
1 cup quick grits
½ teaspoon salt
1½ cups milk
¼ cup butter

1 large clove garlic, peeled, mashed using the side of a knife blade
2 eggs, well beaten, room temperature
1½ cups grated very sharp Cheddar cheese, divided

Preheat oven to 350 degrees.

Bring the water to a boil; add the grits in a steady stream, stirring to blend and avoid lumping. Add in the salt as the grits cook. Stir in the milk, return the mixture just to a boil, lower the heat, and simmer for 5 minutes.

Peel and smash the large garlic clove, using the blade of a large chef's knife. Put the clove under the knife blade and bring your fist down on the blade.

Combine the butter and garlic in a small saucepan over medium heat. Cook just until the garlic becomes aromatic. Remove the garlic clove from the butter and add the butter to the grits, stirring to blend thoroughly.

Beat some of the grits, about a half cup, into the eggs; then turn the eggs into the grits and blend well. Put 1 cup of the cheese into the mixture and stir to blend and melt the cheese. Put the grits into the casserole and top with the reserved cheddar. (If necessary, grate a little more to cover the top.) Put the casserole in the oven and bake until brown around the edges. Yield: 4 – 6 servings.

To the wire first: Charismatic winning the 1999 Kentucky Derby.

Another dish served at many Derby Day brunches is a casserole of grits, good sharp Cheddar cheese, and eggs. It's one of those dishes that bridge the gap between breakfast and lunch, the kind that gave rise to the term brunch. If you're not from the South and you think you don't like grits, this **Cheese Grits Casserole** will change your mind. Its smooth, velvety texture and rich-yet-mild flavor are the winning ticket. And you can feed a lot of people inexpensively with it. If you have leftovers, it's great sliced and sautéed in a little butter.

Another dish even more directly connected to the Kentucky Derby is Derby Pie, a recipe copyrighted by the creator. Like burgoo, there are now dozens, if not hundreds of similar recipes that attempt to re-create the original. Most incorporate two well-known Kentucky products: bourbon and pecans. The pecan tree is native to America, and wild pecans originally grew along the Mississippi River as far north as northern Missouri. Here's one version of **Chocolate Pecan Pie**. See if it satisfies that sweet tooth. This recipe may also be prepared as individual tarts.

And if that's not chocolate enough for

CHOCOLATE PECAN PIE

Crust:
>   **1 cup unbleached flour**
>   **7 tablespoons unsalted butter**
>   **¼ teaspoon salt**
>   **1 – 3 tablespoons ice water**
> **Or use your favorite piecrust**

Filling:
>   **2 eggs**
>   **1 cup sugar**
>   **½ cup melted butter**
>   **¼ cup Kentucky bourbon**
>   **¼ cup cornstarch, sifted**
>   **1 cup toasted, chopped pecans***
>   **1 cup (6 ounces) chopped bittersweet chocolate**

* To toast pecans, spread the nuts in a single layer in a brownie pan and put in a preheated 275-degree oven. When the nuts begin to smell toasty and are slightly browned, they are toasted. Remove and cool.

The crust may be made in a food processor or by hand. If using a processor, put the flour, butter, and salt in the bowl and process until it is the consistency of fine meal. Add 1 tablespoon of ice water at a time and process briefly until the dough starts to form a ball. Remove from the bowl, form into a ball, and roll out on a well-floured board or counter.

If doing it by hand, put the flour, butter, and salt in a large mixing bowl and using a pastry blender or two knives, cut the butter into the flour until it resembles coarse meal. Proceed as above.

Roll out the piecrust and fit into a 9-inch pie plate. Crimp the edges.

Preheat the oven to 350 degrees. For the filling, beat the eggs and sugar in a medium-sized mixing bowl until thick and lemon-colored. Stir in the melted butter, bourbon, and cornstarch. Sprinkle the chopped toasted pecans on the bottom of the piecrust. Sprinkle the chopped chocolate on top of the pecans and pour the egg mixture evenly over the mixed nuts and chocolate. Put in the oven and bake for 45 minutes. Serve slightly warm with unsweetened whipped cream dusted with cocoa, or curls of chocolate. Yield: 8 servings.

KENTUCKY

you, there's always this dessert from Churchill Downs. This is one wickedly wonderful dessert. Called **S'Mores Bread Pudding**, it's comfort food, childhood memories, and a premier artery clogger all in one. That sound you hear is not the drumming of hooves rounding the first turn; it's your arteries snapping shut. Oh, and it's delicious, too.

If this does not satisfy your chocolate craving, absolutely nothing will, ever.

It would not be the Kentucky Derby without the **Mint Julep**. The word julep comes down to us from Persian through Old French (about 1300 or the time of the last Crusades) to Middle English. The Persian original *gulab* means "rosewater." As the word

A mint julep is de rigueur on Derby Day.

DERBY DAY MINT JULEP

1½ cups packed chopped mint
½ cup sugar
1 cup water
Kentucky bourbon
Mint sprigs
Shaved ice
Julep cups or tall glasses

The day before, make the minted simple syrup. Chop the mint, including the stems (much of mint's flavor is in the stems). Put the sugar and water in a small, heavy-bottomed saucepan. Bring to a boil and stir until all the sugar is dissolved; add the mint. Remove from heat, allow the mixture to come to room temperature, and then strain the mixture through clean cheesecloth to remove any bits of cooked mint.

For each julep: take a cup, or tall glass and fill with shaved ice. Pour in a jigger of bourbon and top with the simple syrup; stir gently. Add a sprig or two of mint and serve. Yield: 4 – 6 servings.

moved through time and various languages, it came to mean a sweet syrup in which medicine was frequently disguised. No one would suggest that Kentuckians view their other important product, bourbon, as medicine. Still the name is there. A mint julep is what you drink on Derby Day.

My father made mint juleps only for that one day out of the year. I can still remember my first sip, that exquisite combination of mint, simple syrup, and bourbon. Part of the mystique is the frosted silver Derby julep cup, but you can use frosted glasses just as well. In case you think producing mint juleps for your friends is a lot of work, consider this:

On Derby Day, Churchill Downs uses eighty tons of shaved ice, 7,000 dozen sprigs of mint, and 8,000 liters of mint julep bourbon mix. Go to your kitchen or bar with a light heart and make these up, no matter how many of your friends show up.

Sip your julep, enjoy the Derby pie or the S'Mores, and don't bet the favorite.

CHOCOLATE S'MORES BREAD PUDDING

1 loaf brioche or challah bread
1 quart heavy cream
12 ounces bittersweet chocolate, chopped
½ cup Dutch process cocoa
1 tablespoon vanilla extract
10 eggs
1 teaspoon ground cinnamon
1 cup sugar
½ cup semi-sweet chocolate chips
8 ounces marshmallows

Dice bread into ½-inch cubes and set aside. Generously butter an oven-proof dish at least 2 inches deep — a 9x12x2" works perfectly. Preheat the oven to 300 degrees.

Combine the heavy cream, bittersweet chopped chocolate, cocoa powder, and vanilla in the top of a double boiler over barely simmering water. When the chocolate has melted, remove from the heat and allow the mixture to cool to room temperature. Whisk to blend together.

Beat the eggs with the sugar and cinnamon until they are thick and lemon-colored. Add the egg and cinnamon mixture to the chocolate mixture. Whisk together until completely blended.

Place the brioche or challah in the prepared baking dish. Make sure it reaches the top of the dish.

Pour the chocolate mixture over the brioche and mix thoroughly, using a rubber spatula to turn the mixture gently. Sprinkle chocolate pieces over the bread pudding before placing it in the oven.

Bake at 300 degrees for 35 – 45 minutes, or until the bread pudding sets. The center should be barely firm. Let cool and cut in to desired serving size.

To serve:

Turn on broiler. Cut marshmallows in half lengthwise and place marshmallows on top of bread pudding.

Place the bread pudding with the marshmallows under the broiler; broil until marshmallows are golden brown. Watch closely; as you may remember from campfire days, marshmallows catch fire easily. Top with chocolate sauce, if desired. Yield: 6 – 10 servings, depending on appetite and ability to absorb immense quantities of very rich chocolate.

CHAPTER 5

MID-ATLANTIC

MARYLAND & THE PREAKNESS
DELAWARE & THE DEL 'CAP

Maryland can certainly stake a claim as one of the first locations on this side of the pond to engage actively in horse racing. The Maryland Jockey Club was founded in 1743. Some eighty years after Charles II had served as his own jockey and inaugurated races with rules, horses were being imported from England into the then-colony, according to jockey club records.

But for many Marylanders, and the rest of us who follow the Triple Crown races, it really all began with a dinner party at the Union Hall Hotel in Saratoga Springs, New York, in 1868 (there is no record of the menu). Milton Sanford, whose wealth came from supplying the Union Army with blankets during the Civil War, was the host. During dinner Maryland Governor Odin Bowie proposed to the gentlemen present that their horses, then yearlings, run a race two years hence to commemorate the evening. The winner would have to host the losers for dinner. Both Saratoga and the American Jockey Club at Jamaica Racetrack in New York bid to hold the event, but Bowie pledged that he would build a model racetrack in his home state if the race were run in Baltimore. Thus, Pimlico and the Dinner Party Stakes came into being.

Two years later Sanford's horse, Preakness, won the first running of the Dinner Party Stakes. Sanford had hosted the original dinner party; he now had to host the second, thanks to Preakness. The Dinner Party Stakes evolved into the Dixie Handicap, the eighth-oldest stakes race in the nation. A race for three-year-olds was inaugurated in the spring meet of 1873 at Pimlico and named in honor of Sanford's excellent runner, Preakness. The Preakness predates the Kentucky Derby by two years, making it the second-oldest of the Triple Crown races.

Pimlico is more than just a racetrack. It is a destination for owners and breeders who

Calling the horses to the post in the Preakness Stakes, Maryland's premier sporting event.

MID-ATLANTIC

*Outriders sport special saddle
cloths on race day.*

ARTICHOKE DIP

1 (14-ounce) can artichokes in brine
½ cup freshly grated Parmesan cheese
½ cup good mayonnaise
Dash of cayenne pepper

Preheat the oven to 375 degrees. Drain the artichokes
well. Chop fine and put in an oven-proof dish or casserole
dish. Mix the cheese, mayonnaise, and cayenne pepper.
Add to the artichokes; stir well to blend. Bake for about 30
minutes until the edges are bubbly and slightly browned.
Serve with sliced baguettes or sturdy crackers.
Yield: 4 – 6 servings, depending on appetite.

The Maryland Hunt Cup ranks as one of the state's major equine events.

raise horses on farms in the surrounding countryside and in southeastern Pennsylvania, Delaware, and Virginia. One of those pre-eminent breeders and owners is Allaire du Pont. Everyone on the East Coast and most racing people know Bohemia Stables and Woodstock Farm in Chesapeake City, Maryland. If you know anything at all about racing, you might remember a horse from the 1960s named Kelso. He is the only five-time Horse of the Year. He was also bred and owned by Mrs. du Pont, who knows a thing or two about horses. She also knows a thing or two about food. Here's her recipe for **Artichoke Dip** — infinitely expandable, depending on how many you intend to serve.

This chapter may seem heavy on the seafood, but look at a map. Maryland and Delaware share with Virginia a piece of land called the Delmarva Peninsula. The peninsula provides access to Chesapeake Bay, where the blue crab loves to hang out and the oysters are among

CRAB & POTATO SOUP

3 medium potatoes, peeled & quartered
1 large yellow onion, peeled & quartered
7 cups rich chicken stock
½ pound lump crabmeat, picked over & cartilage removed

For the roux:
  2 tablespoons butter, room temperature
  3 tablespoons flour

1½ teaspoons Old Bay® seasoning
1 cup heavy cream

In a large stockpot, combine the potatoes, onion, and chicken stock. Bring to a boil; reduce the heat, and simmer, covered, for 15 – 20 minutes until the potatoes and onions are soft. Pick over the crabmeat to be sure all the cartilage has been removed. Strain the potatoes and onions, reserving the stock. Put the stock back on the burner on low heat.

Put the potatoes and onions in a food processor and blend until smooth and creamy. You may need to add a half cup or so of the stock. Return the purée to the chicken stock and whisk briskly to incorporate. The soup should be barely simmering at this point.

Make a roux of the butter and flour by mashing them together with a fork in a custard cup. Add to the soup; whisk to incorporate and thicken. Add the crabmeat and the Old Bay® seasoning. At the very last, add the cream and stir long enough to heat through. Garnish each bowl with a generous piece of crabmeat and a pinch of Old Bay®. Yield: 6 servings.

A veteran Preakness-goer.

the world's best. Those are just two of the bay's more prominent denizens, which is why you'll find them, their cousins, and other relatives in such profusion in this chapter.

Now here's a superlative **Crab & Potato Soup** from the Bayard House restaurant in Chesapeake City. This soup is a wonderful way to begin a winter dinner party or a family Sunday supper or just to enjoy crabmeat.

Some of the racetracks featured in this book offer great soups on their menus. Sometimes it's a signature dish, like the Manhattan Clam Chowder at Belmont Park, and sometimes it's just comfort food. Soup is popular at racetracks because a dedicated horseplayer can eat it with-

Black-eyed Susans bedeck the Preakness winner and abound at Pimlico.

PIMLICO CHICKEN NOODLE SOUP

2 tablespoons butter
2 tablespoons olive oil
1 cup diced celery
1 cup diced onions
1 cup diced carrots
1 teaspoon minced fresh garlic
1 cup diced, cooked chicken
1 teaspoon crumbled, dried sage
1 teaspoon lemon pepper
1 tablespoon Worcestershire sauce
1 teaspoon dried mustard
1½ quarts rich chicken broth
½ package (8 ounces) small-type pasta*
1 cup heavy cream
Cornstarch to thicken, if necessary

* Be sure pasta is small. Consider orzo or ditallini. I tested with a bowtie that expanded to life-sized. I had soup you had to cut to eat politely.

Melt the butter in a large stockpot or deep saucepan. Add the oil and then add the celery, onions, carrots, and the fresh garlic. Sauté gently for 10 minutes or until the vegetables are tender and the onions are translucent. Add the chicken after the first 5 minutes and stir to mix in. Add the sage, lemon pepper, Worcestershire sauce, and mustard; stir to blend and cook to incorporate for 5 minutes. Add the chicken broth and pasta and simmer gently for 30 minutes. Remove from the burner and stir in the cream. Return to the burner and heat through. Taste for seasoning. If the soup seems thin, add a tablespoon of cornstarch dissolved in a tablespoon of warm water. Yield: 6 servings.

out having to stop and cut up or butter anything; he or she just eats it while still reading the *Racing Form*. It's quick, nourishing, and in the case of the **Chicken Noodle Soup** at Pimlico, a whole new take on an old favorite. Bet your grandmama's chicken noodle was never like this.

Those fortunate enough to grow up near Chesapeake Bay are as devoted to blue crab as any New Englander ever was to lobster. Crab cakes are one of the manifestations of that

PIMLICO CRAB CAKES

Crab Cake Base:
- ¾ **cup good mayonnaise**
- ¼ **cup Gulden's® mustard**
- 1 **teaspoon Tabasco® sauce**
- 1 **teaspoon Worcestershire sauce**
- 1 **egg, well beaten**

- 1 **pound fresh jumbo lump crabmeat**
- 1 **cup fresh bread crumbs***

- 3 **tablespoons butter**
- 4 **tablespoons light olive oil**

* Make from scratch or buy the best quality bread crumbs you can find. Panko, or Japanese bread crumbs, don't get soggy and work well in this recipe.

In a small mixing bowl, mix together the mayonnaise, mustard, Tabasco®, Worcestershire sauce, and well-beaten egg. Blend well so the base is smooth. Set aside.

Put the crabmeat in a large bowl and pick over carefully and gently to remove any stray bits of shell or cartilage. Add the bread crumbs first and then the base; stir gently to combine and form the crab cakes, using your hands and patting the cakes into an oblong shape. Don't make them too thick or they'll fall apart when you're sautéing them.

In a large sauté pan, melt the butter and light olive oil and sauté the cakes gently until they are brown on both sides, about 5 minutes per side. Drain briefly on paper towels and serve at once. Yield: 6 (4-ounce) cakes.

love, and naturally Pimlico serves them. On Preakness Day the track will dish up 14,000 or so of its **Pimlico Crab Cakes**.

This is a pretty basic crab cake recipe that you can easily experiment with if you're feeling adventuresome. You could add chopped scallions or parsley to the mix, delete the mustard and add lemon grass, or add some curry. Let your taste buds dictate and have some fun! You could also make much smaller cakes and serve them at a cocktail party or make mid-sized cakes and serve them as an appetizer at a dinner party. Versatility is the word.

WILD RICE RING

1 pound long-grain wild rice	¼ cup finely chopped red pimentos
4 cups chicken stock or 4 cups water with 2 chicken bouillon cubes	½ cup fresh or frozen green peas
¼ cup finely chopped onion	1 cup good mayonnaise
¼ cup chopped celery	1 tablespoon olive oil

Put the wild rice in a large, heavy-bottomed saucepan with the chicken stock or water and bouillon cubes. Bring to a boil and simmer for about 50 – 60 minutes or until the rice is tender. You may add more liquid if needed. Drain.

Put the rice in a large mixing bowl. Add the onion, celery, pimentos, and green peas. Toss to blend well. Stir in the mayonnaise.

Use the olive oil to grease a 10-inch ring mold or bundt pan. Place the rice mixture in the mold, tamping it down evenly all around. Be careful as you don't want any holes. Place plastic wrap on the rice mixture to seal. Refrigerate for at least 1 hour.

When you are ready to serve it, prepare a platter with lettuce or other leafy greens. Remove the mold from the refrigerator. Carefully remove the plastic wrap and invert the mold onto the platter and pull up evenly so the rice ring comes out in one piece. Slice and serve. Yield: 6 – 8 servings.

Here's another of Mrs. du Pont's recipes, this one a perfect accompaniment to an entrée of grilled steak or roast chicken. Her **Wild Rice Ring** would be good in the summer, too, with the addition of some cooked chicken or salmon, finely diced. However you serve it, it's good. Just be sure when you purchase your wild rice that you don't buy paddy-grown. If the rice is paddy-grown, it must be labeled as such. It tends to have a slightly muddy taste instead of that wonderful nutty, grassy taste of true wild rice.

Mrs. du Pont remains one of racing's most enthusiastic boosters. When asked once about her most exciting moment in horse racing, she

Allaire C. du Pont and her illustrious champion Kelso.

MID-ATLANTIC

replied: "Every single moment; every single race. Every race is more exciting than the one before it. "

DELAWARE PARK AND THE DEL 'CAP

Like its sister state of Maryland, Delaware was active in horse racing during the Colonial period. The state's first formal racing facility was built in Newark in 1760. From then until the Depression, county fairs kept racing alive in Delaware.

In 1936 the newly created Delaware Racing Commission met with the Delaware Steeplechase and Race Association. The association, made up of five area businessmen, had formed to "promote the breeding of the Thoroughbred horse and the establishment of a racetrack."

The upshot was the creation of Delaware Park, designed by William du Pont Jr., who already had designed twenty-three racecourses. The track was a one-mile dirt oval with two

steeplechase courses and a 7,500-seat open-air grandstand for the patrons. A 1958 remodeling expanded the seating area, enlarged the clubhouse, and added closed-circuit televisions and a winner's circle. During Delaware Park's early years, fans came on the Pennsylvania and B&O railroads to a terminal near the track. In addition, buses ran from Philadelphia, Baltimore, and Wilmington.

By 1985 Delaware Park, like many other tracks, was in trouble. It was taken over by William Rickman Sr., a local

Delaware Park has undergone changes over the years, but its Delaware Handicap remains a prestigious test of fillies and mares. Princess Turia (above) wins the 1957 version of the race.

real estate developer who was determined to set it back on its feet. Promotion of the track's attractive picnic grove along the rail, the return of the Delaware Handicap, simulcasting, and the initiation of the Twin Trifecta wager were all steps taken to preserve and promote racing in Delaware. In 1994 the Delaware legislature passed the Horse Racing Redevelopment Act, permitting the installation of video slots at Delaware racetracks.

Delaware Park, now able to offer increasingly larger purses, saw an influx of top-flight horses. The Delaware Handicap, the track's premier race, again welcomed the country's top race mares and fillies to compete for a purse of $600,000. Billed as the "Race of the Classic Dam," the 'Cap has been won by the dams of Graustark, Easy Goer, Go for Wand, Gulch, and Forward Pass. If Thoroughbred breeding is your game, this race is the place to spot future classic dams; if you're just a fan, it's a great race to watch some of the best race mares in the country compete.

While deciding which filly to back, order **Angels on Horseback** and see whether that

The paddock at Delaware Park is one of the track's most picturesque spots.

helps bring insight. Angels on Horseback is an appetizer on the menu in Delaware Park's restaurants — those angels would be the winning jockeys in any horseplayer's mind, but here they are oysters.

They are also called "Pigs in Blankets," although the Angels name is older and comes from England. In attempting to track down the origins of both dish and name, the reference librarian at the Schlesinger Library at Radcliffe, which is the country's premier culinary library, drew a blank. Pigs in Blankets have also come to signify small hot dogs baked in puff pastry and served with a cocktail sauce or mustard. But the Angels name is unsullied and remains firmly attached to the oyster wrapped in bacon and grilled as so given.

It should also be noted that Angels on Horseback is the title of one of the most delightful books on the subject of children and ponies. Written and illustrated by Norman Thelwell, it is a must-have if you have young children who are horse/pony mad.

It seems appropriate somehow that Delaware Park

ANGELS ON HORSEBACK

1 cup flour, seasoned with salt & freshly ground black pepper
1 dozen fresh oysters
12 strips lean bacon
Toothpicks

Preheat the oven to 450 degrees. Place a rack in a shallow roasting pan.

Put the flour, salt, and pepper in a shallow bowl and mix well. Lightly dredge the oysters in the flour; wrap a strip of bacon around each, secure with a toothpick, and place on the rack. When all the oysters are thus dressed, put the pan in the oven and cook until the bacon crisps. Turn once to be sure bacon crisps evenly. Watch to be sure the bacon does not burn. Serve immediately.

Yield: 2 servings.

CLAMS CASINO DELAWARE PARK

12 medium hard shell clams, shucked, bottom shells reserved
½ green bell pepper, finely diced
½ red bell pepper, finely diced
1 medium onion, finely diced
4 slices bacon, finely diced
Extra bacon, cut in ½-inch squares

Open clams; place each clam on half-shell in a shallow oven-proof baking pan that will accommodate all the clams. (A layer of coarse salt will balance shells.) Preheat the oven to 400 degrees.

Put the peppers, onion, and finely diced bacon in a skillet and cook over medium-high heat for 5 – 7 minutes, stirring to be sure ingredients don't stick to the pan.

Remove the pan from the heat, drain the ingredients briefly on paper towels, and top each opened clam with the mixture. Place uncooked bacon square on each clam.

Put the dish in the oven and cook 12 – 15 minutes until just cooked through. Serve at once. Yield: 12 clams or enough for 1 hungry person, 2 of moderate appetite.

OYSTER SCALLOP — CRÈME FRAICHE

36 oysters
Cream Sauce:
  1½ cups milk
  1½ cups light cream
  2 thin slices of onion
  1 clove
  ½ bay leaf
  ⅛ teaspoon freshly grated nutmeg

For the roux:
  4 tablespoons butter
  4 tablespoons unbleached flour
  ½ teaspoon salt
  ⅛ teaspoon white pepper

1 cup small bread cubes
1 cup cooked, diced chicken
½ cup buttered bread crumbs
½ cup (about 2 ounces) grated Gruyere cheese

Make the cream sauce:

First, place the milk and cream in a heavy-bottomed pan with the sliced onion, bay leaf, clove, and the grating of nutmeg. Scald over medium-high heat. That is, bring just to the boiling point and remove from the heat. Strain the milk-cream mixture and discard the seasonings.

In another pan, melt the butter and whisk in the flour. Stir to blend and cook a little. Do not allow to brown. Add the milk-cream mixture all at once to the roux, stirring constantly until the mixture is thickened and smooth. Add the salt and pepper.

Preheat the oven to 325 degrees. Generously butter a 2-quart oven-proof casserole and arrange half the oysters on the bottom. Sprinkle ¼ cup of the bread cubes over them and pour 1 cup of the cream sauce over all.

Place all the diced chicken in the second layer; top with another ¼ cup of the bread cubes and the remaining oysters and then the rest of the bread cubes. Mix the bread crumbs and cheese together and sprinkle over the top. Bake in the preheated oven till well-browned on top. Serve at once. Yield: 6 servings.

should also offer its version of **Clams Casino** on the menu. Try this for a winning appetizer.

Thoroughbred owners and breeders are plentiful in the Mid-Atlantic region, and there is always cause for entertaining clients, associates, and friends, ideally to celebrate victory by a homebred runner in a stakes race at Delaware Park. This next recipe comes from Elizabeth Moran, who owns Brushwood Stables in Malvern, Pennsylvania. "It's one of those family recipes that is just 'made' and the proportions had to be figured out!" said Moran. The recipe is called **Oyster Scallop — Crème Fraiche**, not because there is crème fraiche in the dish but because Moran campaigned a horse named Crème Fraiche who won the 1985

Belmont Stakes, along with a lot of other races. He is also one of a select company of horses that won the Jockey Club Gold Cup in back-to-back years. About him, she says, "Crème Fraiche was so named because he is by Rich Cream out of Likely Exchange. Hence, a bit of cream that can take a beating…but it wasn't too often that he was beaten. The cream always rises to the top!" Crème Fraiche still resides at Moran's farm.

One of our testers could find only canned oysters when it was time to test, and she reports that the scallop was absolutely delicious. If you can't find the fresh or they are out of season, you can use canned. Remember that in the past, oysters were packed in barrels of damp sand and shipped via the railroads to the Midwest where they became a staple of Christmas Eve suppers in oyster stew. So they pack and travel well for dishes such as this one.

After a winning summer afternoon at the races, what better way to ease into evening than with dinner at downtown Wilmington's best restaurant, 821, so named because of its location at 821 Market Street. Chef Tobias Lawry, who obviously knows a thing or two about seafood, serves up his delicious **Grilled Soft Shell Crab & Summer Vegetable Salad**.

Another winning main course comes from Gretchen Jackson, who was a classmate of

---

GRILLED SOFT SHELL CRAB & SUMMER VEGETABLE SALAD

40 spears asparagus
4 ears corn, shucked
¼ cup fresh lemon juice
¼ cup minced fresh mint leaves
¼ cup minced fresh basil leaves
¼ cup minced fresh flat-leaf parsley leaves
1 cup olive oil
⅛ cup minced fresh tarragon leaves
Salt & freshly ground pepper to taste
8 soft shell crabs
2 tablespoons olive oil
2 tablespoons honey
Salt & freshly ground black pepper

Light your grill. Clean the asparagus. Coat the asparagus and the corn with half the lemon juice and olive oil seasoned with salt & pepper. Place on the grill. Cook until slightly charred, about 2 – 3 minutes for the asparagus, slightly longer for the corn. Cut the asparagus into bite-sized pieces and place in a mixing bowl. Cut the corn off the cob into the same bowl.

Allow the mixture to cool. Add the remaining lemon juice and olive oil. Season the salad with salt and pepper to taste. Add in the fresh herbs. Toss to blend well. Set the salad aside.

Season the soft shell crabs with the olive oil, salt, and pepper. Grill on a medium-hot spot of the grill, turning twice and flipping over once until cooked through but still nice and juicy. Pull off the grill. Put the salad on 8 service plates; put the crabs on the salad. Slightly warm the honey and drizzle over the crabs. Serve. Yield: 8 servings.

CHICKEN BELLE CHERIE

Flour
4 chicken breasts, skinned, boned, halved
3 large garlic cloves, finely chopped
**5 tablespoons butter or 2 tablespoons butter
& 3 of canola or other good cooking oil**
6 – 8 plum tomatoes, sliced crosswise
1 green bell pepper, seeded, julienned
¼ cup chopped fresh basil
½ cup grated fresh mozzarella
Salt & freshly ground pepper to taste

Pound the chicken breasts to make them flat. Dredge the chicken breasts in the flour; shake off excess. Heat the butter, or butter and oil (the oil will keep the butter from smoking) in a large sauté pan. Add the chicken breasts to the pan and sprinkle the chopped garlic over all. Brown the chicken on both sides, cover the pan, reduce the heat, and cook the chicken until it is fork tender, about 20 minutes.

Add the tomatoes, pepper, and fresh basil and cook until everything is heated through. Do not overcook or the vegetables will become mushy. Sprinkle the mozzarella on the chicken and allow it to melt. Serve immediately over rice or pasta. Arrange the peppers and tomatoes around the chicken breasts on the plate. Yield: 4 servings.

mine in school, never mind how long ago. I knew she was involved in racing; I had been out to her farm in Chester County, Pennsylvania, and met some of her horses. She even owned, briefly, a horse named Guthrie. So when I was asked to put this book together I naturally contacted her to see how she was doing and if she'd like to contribute. Since she raised four kids, in addition to all the horses, I was pretty sure she knew how to cook. She contributed this recipe, **Chicken Belle Cherie**, which she says goes together in about thirty minutes. I tried it and she's right. I cooked a pot full of rice at the same time, and the chicken was perfect over that. It's also delicious.

Her recipe is dedicated to her race mare Belle Cherie, who won four graded stakes in her racing career, running on both the turf and dirt.

I first encountered rice pudding on the menu at Delaware Park, and it seemed an odd dessert for a horse racing venue. Then I saw it again on other racetrack restaurant menus. In thinking about it, I realized rice pudding is a comfort food from childhood, and each of us has certainly had at least one day at the track when we needed comfort to a childish degree. Here's a good, old-fashioned **Rice Pudding** made the way you wish your grandmother had made it.

One of the testers, who is cholesterol-challenged, tried this rice pudding using skim milk and egg substitutes made from egg whites. It was just as good, just as creamy, and much better for those who must watch their fat intake. The secret seems to be in the long cooking

RICE PUDDING

¼ cup raisins	¼ cup sugar
1 tablespoon Grand Marnier liqueur	½ cup milk
2¾ cups whole milk	¼ teaspoon ground mace
½ cup white rice	1 teaspoon orange zest*
⅛ teaspoon salt	1 tablespoon honey
3 eggs	

* When a recipe calls for the zest of citrus fruit, I recommend that you use organically raised fruit. Citrus are some of the most heavily sprayed fruits grown commercially and their skin, like ours, has pores.

Put the raisins in a small bowl and pour the Grand Marnier over them; stir and set aside at least 1 hour ahead of making the pudding. They may be soaked overnight.

In the top of a double boiler, over just-simmering water, put a half cup of the milk, the rice, and the salt together. Stir to wet the grains of rice. Keep the water just simmering and stir the rice occasionally. As the milk is absorbed add another half cup and stir to blend. Keep adding the milk until it is all absorbed and the rice is plump and tender. Remove from the heat.

Preheat the oven to 300 degrees. Grease a 2-quart oven-proof casserole. Beat the eggs with the sugar until thick and lemon-colored. Beat in the milk, mace, orange zest, and honey. Add in the raisins. Stir the egg mixture into the rice and pour into the casserole. Put the casserole into the oven and bake for 30 minutes or until the pudding is set. Yield: 6 servings.

and absorbing process.

Racing to the table in the Mid-Atlantic region brings you racing history, plenty of excellent seafood, and good, old-fashioned comfort food but, regretfully, no hot tips.

A private barn at Delaware Park.

CHAPTER 6

NEW YORK

NEW YORK

BELMONT PARK & SARATOGA

Racing has always been big in New York, nowhere more so than at Belmont Park. The most expansive track in American racing, Belmont also features the longest and last race of the Triple Crown. The Belmont Stakes is run at a mile and a half, a challenging race for a three-year-old, especially one that has already competed in the Kentucky Derby and the Preakness Stakes.

First run in 1867 and named for August Belmont, the Belmont Stakes is the oldest Triple Crown event and the fourth oldest stakes race in North America. The race was run at the now defunct Jerome and Morris parks before being moved to Belmont Park for that track's opening in 1905. August Belmont's son, August II, was head of the Westchester Racing Association when the track was built between 1903 and 1905. Then the most expensive and grandiose track in America, Belmont Park opened May 4, 1905, with 40,000 fans in attendance. The track was large enough for the Wright Brothers to supervise an international aerial tournament in 1910. In 1918 the track served as the first New York terminal for airmail service between Washington, D.C., and New York City.

Sir Barton won the first Triple Crown in 1919, although he was not acknowledged as the first Triple Crown winner until 1930 when sportswriter Charlie Hatton coined the phrase in connection with Gallant Fox's three wins. Gallant Fox further distinguished himself later in his life by becoming the only Triple Crown winner to sire a Triple Crown winner, Omaha. The 1977 Triple Crown winner Seattle Slew came close when his son Swale won two of the three in 1984.

Highly acclaimed, the Triple Crown is one of the most difficult goals to achieve in sports. Only eleven colts have managed to win all three races, the last, Affirmed, in 1978. There are forty-six near misses, colts that have won two of the three but just couldn't quite put it all to-

The paddock at Belmont Park has witnessed the saddling of many a superstar.

When it opened in 1905, Belmont Park was the costliest and most grandiose track in America.

gether. Native Dancer, Northern Dancer, Damascus, Swale, Silver Charm, Charismatic, and Point Given have all come close and earned year-end championship titles in their quest.

Since its inception, Belmont Park has held races integral in determining which horses become champions.

Much less well known is the integral role Belmont played in burgoo's being available at the food service stands throughout Keeneland racetrack's grandstand. It happened this way: One of the men responsible for running Keeneland was attending the Belmont Stakes and noticed that the track's signature Manhattan Clam Chowder was available everywhere, not just in the track's white tablecloth restaurant. When he returned to Lexington, he spoke to the food manager, Larry Wolken, and asked if Keeneland could do the same thing with the burgoo. That's why today you can get burgoo anywhere food is served at Keeneland. And here is the dish, as they serve it at Belmont, that brought it to you.

This is **Manhattan Clam Chowder Belmont Park**, redolent of clams and the spices that

Turf racing long has been a tradition at Belmont, which has served as host to three Breeders' Cup championship days.

MANHATTAN CLAM CHOWDER BELMONT PARK

2 tablespoons butter
2 tablespoons oil
2 ribs celery, finely chopped
1 small onion, finely chopped
½ green or red bell pepper, finely chopped
1 (14½-ounce) can tomatoes, drained
1½ tablespoons tomato paste

1 teaspoon paprika
1 teaspoon dried thyme
1 teaspoon curry powder
1 teaspoon minced fresh garlic
1 cup diced Yukon Gold potatoes
1 pound clams
1 (8-ounce) bottle clam juice
Salt & freshly ground pepper to taste

Drain the tomatoes, strain the juice to remove the seeds, and reserve. In a small saucepan, boil the potatoes until they are just fork tender. In a large soup pot, over medium heat, sauté the celery, onion, and pepper in the butter and oil until the vegetables are tender and the onion translucent, about 10 minutes. Add in the tomatoes and strained juice. Add the paprika, thyme, curry powder, and garlic. Cook for 2 minutes. Add in the cooked potatoes and their water. Cook another 3 minutes at a simmer. Add in the clams, their juices, and the bottled clam juice. Bring to a boil, reduce the heat, and simmer gently. Add in the tomato paste. Add salt and pepper to taste, if necessary. Yield: 1½ quarts.

NEW YORK

HERB-STUFFED MUSHROOMS

1 pound medium-large mushrooms, stems removed
¼ cup finely diced cooked ham
1 teaspoon oregano
¼ teaspoon thyme
Salt & freshly ground black pepper to taste
1 teaspoon finely chopped flat-leaf parsley
2 tablespoons freshly grated Parmesan cheese
2 tablespoons good bread crumbs
Olive oil

Remove the stems from the mushrooms and chop fine. Pour a little of the olive oil in a custard cup. One by one, dip the mushrooms in the oil and place the caps in a shallow baking pan. Preheat the oven to 350 degrees.

When the oven is hot, put the mushroom caps in the oven and bake for 15 minutes. Turn them over and bake another 10 minutes. Remove from the oven and let them cool until they are easily handled.

Put the chopped mushroom stems in mixing bowl with the ham, herbs, cheese, and bread crumbs. Mix well until all the ingredients are completely blended. Add a bit of the olive oil to hold the stuffing together if necessary. Stuff the mushroom caps with the mixture. Put a drop or two of olive oil on each mushroom cap and put the pan in the oven. Bake just long enough to heat all the way through. They should be good and hot. Yield: 6 – 8 for cocktails.

give it a hearty taste and heft. It's a wonderful soup for a midwinter's evening or when you missed a trifecta by a nose. This recipe convinced me Manhattan Clam Chowder should be in everyone's chowder lexicon. I had never been a fan, but this one made me a convert.

Chowders are an American dish. They first appeared in the seventeenth century and were made from fish, onions, and hardtack, that tough, seagoing version of bread. Gradually, cream and butter were added, and then lean salt pork. The word may have come to us through the French word *chaudiere*, which means "cauldron," or it may have come from an English term in use in Cornwall and Devon for fishmonger: jowter or chowter.

There is another old phrase, "one thing leads to another." In doing this book, I encountered one horse-loving cook who led to another and another and made my task easy, entertaining, and just plain fun. I met Betty and Len Powell through Primrose Hayes, a neighboring breeder who was introduced to me by Anne and Joe McMahon, whom you'll meet a little bit further on. Betty grew up on a New York dairy farm and always had horses. She acquired a trainer's license for Standardbred horses when she was just eighteen. More recently Betty has served on the board of the New York Thoroughbred Breeders Association and worked as an agent at sales. Betty and Len have been active in the New York breeding scene for a long time. They entertain often, and from those experiences Betty shares some great, easy recipes, including one for **Herb-Stuffed Mushrooms**.

Stuffed mushroom caps have been around for a long time and have lost none of their tasty appeal. This recipe makes enough for a small cocktail party or an appetizer for a family dinner.

Here's a main dish, **Flounder Roll Ups**, from Betty that is easy to prepare, can be done a bit ahead, and should be refrigerated until ready to bake. It's delicious. I wish I could have tried the recipe with Betty's special ingredient. According to Primrose Hayes, Len grows his own cayenne peppers, which he dries and then grinds in a small coffee bean grinder. Primrose says, "Betty's a good cook, but Len's hot pepper seasoning makes her food shine." So if you've got a Len in your circle, use his or her paprika on the fish and make it shine.

This flounder would be great with just a salad and some good, crusty rolls. And an excellent dessert to follow, of course.

The McMahons and one of the farm's stallions.

FLOUNDER ROLL UPS

8 fillets (6 – 8 ounces) of flounder, or other good white fish
⅓ cup butter, melted
⅓ cup fresh lemon juice
2 chicken bouillon cubes
1 teaspoon Tabasco® sauce
Paprika
1 cup cooked rice
1 (10-ounce) package frozen chopped broccoli, drained
1 cup shredded cheddar cheese

Preheat the oven to 350 degrees. In a saucepan melt the butter, add the lemon juice, bouillon cubes, and Tabasco® sauce. Continue cooking over low heat until the bouillon cubes have melted. Stir to blend well. Set the sauce aside.

In a mixing bowl combine the cooked rice, chopped and drained broccoli, and grated cheese and then add ¼ cup of the lemon butter sauce. Stir to blend completely.

Lay the fillets out in a shallow baking dish. Divide the filling evenly among the pieces of fish; then roll up each fillet and place seam side down in the pan. Pour the remaining sauce over the fish. Sprinkle with paprika and bake for 20 – 25 minutes until the fish is cooked through. Yield: 8 servings.

The McMahons' breeding business, McMahon of Saratoga Thoroughbreds, is very much a part of the New York racing scene. Anne McMahon writes, "We had the good fortune to move here (Saratoga Springs and a two hundred-plus-year-old farm) in 1971. We had chickens, pigs, and a garden. Gradually the horse business grew and supported us and then turned into a big business, but I have such fond memories of the old days." Anne and Joe have substantially expanded the business in recent years to provide room for any of their interested children, and three of the five have joined up so far. McMahon of Saratoga Thoroughbreds now stands eight stallions and was expecting one hundred foals on the ground in 2002.

The McMahon farm is very much a part of the New York racing scene.

Having raised five hungry kids, Anne's a cook who knows the basics. Here's her recipe for **Pineapple Upside Down Cake**. Pineapple upside down cake first appeared in cookbooks about 1920, around the time canned pineapple became widely available. Sometimes referred to back then as pineapple skillet cake, it's best made in a cast-iron skillet or frying pan, although any other pan will do if you aren't fortunate enough to own "Mom's old skillet."

This is great Sunday night supper fare or on a weeknight as a special treat. It works equally well as a take-along to a potluck or covered-dish supper. It looks good on a brunch buffet, too, and tastes even better than it looks.

Anne's correspondence with me about recipes is somewhat heavy on the dessert side. I couldn't resist her recipe for **McMahon Pumpkin Pie**.

It is legitimate to purchase the pumpkins for your pie at a farm stand, if you don't have

PINEAPPLE UPSIDE DOWN CAKE

"Your mom's old cast-iron skillet"*

1 stick unsalted butter
1 cup brown sugar
Canned pineapple slices, in juice
Candied cherries (optional)
6 tablespoons butter, softened
1 cup sugar
2 eggs
1 teaspoon vanilla extract
1 tablespoon dark rum
1½ cups flour
2 teaspoons baking powder
½ cup unsweetened pineapple juice**

* Can also be made in a 9x13x2" pan.
** Use the juice from the canned pineapple.

Melt the stick of butter in "Mom's pan" or in the brownie pan. Add the brown sugar and stir to blend completely so mixture is smooth and uniform. Place the slices of pineapple in the pan; put a cherry in the center of each slice, if desired. Set aside but keep warm.

Preheat the oven to 350 degrees. In a large mixing bowl, using an electric mixer or by hand, whip the butter and sugar together until fluffy. Add in the eggs, vanilla extract, and rum; beat to incorporate.

Sift the flour and baking powder together. Add the flour mixture alternately with the pineapple juice to the batter until everything is incorporated and the batter is smooth. Pour the batter into the pan on top of the pineapple slices and put in the oven. Bake for 35 – 40 minutes or until the cake pulls away slightly from the sides of the pan and is slightly springy to the touch. Remove from the oven and allow the cake to cool slightly. Place the serving platter over the pan; invert the pan, and the cake should exit gracefully onto the platter. Serve warm with unsweetened whipped cream or plain. Yield: 6 servings.

McMAHON PUMPKIN PIE

First grow or buy a pie pumpkin. Slice it in half, scoop out the seeds, and place the halves on a baking sheet and bake at 350 degrees until fork tender. Let the pumpkin cool to room temperature, scoop out the soft insides, and measure into the blender or the bowl of a food processor. For 1½ cups of pumpkin:

¾ cup sugar
½ teaspoon salt
1 teaspoon cinnamon
½ teaspoon ginger
¼ teaspoon ground cloves
¼ teaspoon nutmeg
3 eggs
1¼ cups whole milk (or half & half)

Preheat the oven to 400 degrees. Put all the ingredients in the bowl of a food processor or in a blender. Blend together until smooth and thick. You may want to decrease the amount of milk or light cream slightly as this filling is generous. Pour the mixture into an unbaked pie shell. You can decorate the top of the pie using your favorite cookie cutter and leftover bits of pie crust. (I actually have a great turkey cookie cutter.)

Put the pie in the oven and bake for 50 minutes or until a knife inserted into the center of the pie comes out clean.

Yield: 6 – 8 servings.

NEW YORK

room to grow them. Pumpkin vines ramble and take an amazing amount of space, so you need a large farm or at least an acre of ground to grow them if you want to grow other things as well. And, yes, fresh pumpkin does taste better than canned, believe it or not. Try it, and you'll see.

SARATOGA, HORSE RACING, & THE SARATOGA CHIP

Saratoga comes from the Iroquois Indian word *sarachtogue*, which means "hillside of a great river." It was a favored hunting ground of that tribe, which also valued the medicinal properties of its springs. The Iroquois roamed the woods of what is now central and northern New York. Early notables who visited the area include George Washington, Daniel

Known as the "graveyard of champions," Saratoga has caused the undoing of many great horses, such as Gallant Fox to the longshot Jim Dandy.

Webster, Martin Van Buren, and Washington Irving.

They were followed by an influx of New York's wealthiest, who sought surcease from the summer's heat. Vanderbilts, Whitneys, and Rockefellers came, loved it, and made it a summer destination. By the time horse racing was initiated in the 1860s, Saratoga was an established resort famed for its mineral waters and casinos. Diamond Jim Brady and his great pal Lillian Russell were regular visitors to the resort, its restaurants, and its racetrack.

Food is as integral to Saratoga's history as are the horses. The track, established in the days of multi-course meals, enjoyed the patronage of Brady, who began every meal with several dozen Lynnhaven oysters. Seafood dealers along the Chesapeake Bay were so familiar with Diamond Jim's appetite that barrels conveying the largest oysters would be marked on the outside "For Diamond Jim Brady." Some of those barrels made their way to Saratoga during the racing season.

To horse racing fans, Saratoga is an instantly recognized name, a place synonymous with the best in Thoroughbred racing. It should be a name recognized by every single American because it was here that the potato chip, originally the Saratoga chip, that ubiquitous, very American food, was invented at the same time organized racing was establishing itself in town.

According to legend, a chef named George Crum, the son of a mulatto jockey who had come north from New Orleans for the races and a Mohican Indian mother, was directly, or indirectly responsible for the chip.

Crum, a well-known guide and game chef, had been hired to cook at Moon's Lake House, a newly opened resort. Also well known for his prickly personality, Crum one day became increasingly infuriated as a finicky guest kept sending French fried potatoes back to the kitchen, saying they weren't crispy enough. Finally, Crum sliced some potatoes paper-thin, dropped them first in ice water then in hot fat, and sent them, fried to a crisp and heavily salted, out to the table.

His triumph backfired because the guest loved them, and the Saratoga chips, now known as potato chips, became a part of American culinary history. It's reported that by the next day, Saratoga chips were on every table in the resort. However, the chips had to wait seventy-five years for the development of airtight packaging before their distribution became nationwide because they wilt so easily.

NEW YORK

Racing at Saratoga is nirvana for Thoroughbred fans.

As potato chips made their inaugural appearance in Saratoga, so did Thoroughbred racing. August 3–6, 1863, marked the dates of Saratoga's first race meet, put on by John "Old Smoke" Morrissey, a gambler, casino owner, ex-boxing champion, and future Congressman. It's believed that the first meet was held on the "old course" or the track where trotting races were held in Saratoga's early days.

That same August, Morrissey asked three friends, John R. Hunter, William Travers, and Leonard Jerome, to form the Saratoga Association to promote Thoroughbred racing at the "Spa." In 1864 Travers became the track's first president. He instituted a four-day meet and included a stakes race, which is still run today, named in his honor. The Travers, also known as the Midsummer Derby, early on became a race in which the favorite often was beaten, contributing to

Early mornings at Saratoga have a magical quality.

Saratoga's reputation as the "graveyard of champions."

The Travers' most notable "failure" was probably Gallant Fox's loss to 100-1 longshot Jim Dandy. In 1982 the respective winners of the Kentucky Derby (Gato Del Sol), Preakness (Aloma's Ruler), and Belmont Stakes (Conquistador Cielo) met in the Travers, which is still the centerpiece of the Saratoga race meeting. They all lost to Runaway Groom, a Canadian-bred colt with a modest record.

Other notables who have lost here: Secretariat to Onion in the Whitney Handicap; Davona Dale to It's in the Air in the Alabama Stakes; and Man o' War to Upset in the Sanford Stakes. With names like those in the runner-up column, it's easy to see how Saratoga's

ROASTED RACK OF LAMB WITH ROSEMARY JUS

2 racks domestic lamb, trimmed by butcher
Salt & freshly ground black pepper
1 tablespoon minced shallot
1 teaspoon minced garlic
2 tablespoons olive oil
2 cups merlot
2 cups veal demi-glace*
1 teaspoon arrowroot
2 tablespoons fresh rosemary leaves

* Demi-glace is a rich brown sauce that combines veal (or beef) stock with madeira or sherry. It is slowly cooked until reduced by half to a thick glaze that coats a spoon.

Remove the fat cap from the lamb racks, leaving a thin layer of fat on top of the meat. Clean the fat and skin from the chop bones and wrap them in aluminum foil to protect them from scorching. Cut the racks in half, which should give you 4 four-bone servings.

Preheat the oven to 350 degrees. Heat a large skillet over high heat; season the racks with the salt and pepper and sear, fat side down in the hot skillet until well browned. Turn the racks fat side up and place in the oven for about 30 minutes. (You can use a probe thermometer to check internal temperature.) When the racks are the desired temperature, depending on whether you like rare, medium-rare, or well-done meat, remove from the oven and allow to rest for five minutes (160 degrees is usually medium.).

While the lamb is roasting, heat a heavy-bottomed saucepan over medium-high heat and sauté the shallots and garlic in a little olive oil until soft. Add the merlot and turn the heat down to medium. Cook until the merlot is reduced by half.

In another saucepan, heat the demi-glace and allow it to simmer for 20 minutes. Begin stirring in the merlot mixture a little at a time until you can just begin to taste the wine in the sauce. Add in the rosemary leaves. Mix the arrowroot with a little water and add in, stirring to combine. This will give the sauce a bit of thickening and a shine. Season the sauce with salt and pepper.

To serve, ladle the sauce onto four warm plates, cut each lamb piece in half, arrange on the plate, and serve with the roasted garlic bread pudding, sautéed wild mushrooms, and a seasonal green salad. Yield: 4 servings.

reputation arose.

Owners of beaten favorites frequently retire to Siro's to assuage their sorrows. Open only six weeks a year, this revered Saratoga dining institution has to have something powerful going for it. Must be the food. Here's an entrée of **Roasted Rack of Lamb with Rosemary Jus** and **Roasted Garlic Bread Pudding** from executive chef K.D. Maceachron that hints at the reason for the reputation. Plan to dine there when that longshot you backed in the sixth race figures out his mission and pulls away by four and a half lengths.

The bread pudding part of the recipe needs to be started a day or so ahead. The bread pudding "muffins" could even be finished ahead of time and gently reheated.

With such a meal, only a simple salad of the freshest greens is needed. Good coffee and maybe port for dessert.

ROASTED GARLIC BREAD PUDDING

4 cups sourdough bread, crusts removed,
   cut into 1-inch cubes
1 head garlic, roasted
1 cup milk
¼ cup plus 2 tablespoons olive oil
½ cup chopped onion
¼ cup chopped celery
¼ cup chopped carrot

¼ cup chopped red bell pepper
½ green onion, chopped
½ tablespoon minced garlic
½ tablespoon chopped fresh rosemary
2 pints heavy cream
4 whole eggs
1 egg, separated
Salt & freshly ground black pepper to taste

Cut the bread into cubes, spread out, and allow them to dry overnight.

To roast the garlic, cut the tops off the garlic bulbs and simmer in the milk for 10 minutes. Drain, season the garlic with salt and pepper, and combine with ¾ cup olive oil in a tightly covered, small roasting pan and roast for 2 hours in a 275 degree oven. Remove, uncover, and let cool.

Strain the oil to remove any unwanted garlic skins and reserve. Squeeze the garlic from the bulbs and place them in a small food processor or blender and purée, adding the strained oil in a slow, steady stream to emulsify the oil into the purée.

Set a skillet or sauté pan over medium heat and add 2 tablespoons olive oil. When hot, add the onion, celery, carrot, bell pepper, green onion, and minced garlic. Cook until the vegetables begin to soften, about 10 minutes. Mince the rosemary and rub briefly in your hand to release the oils before adding to the vegetables. Cook for another 2 minutes, remove from heat, season with salt and pepper, and allow to cool.

Combine the whole eggs with the egg yolk in a large mixing bowl and beat well. Stir in the heavy cream and the roasted garlic purée until well blended. Combine the cream mixture with the vegetables and the dried bread cubes and mix well. Cover the bowl with plastic wrap and refrigerate overnight. Cover the reserved egg white and refrigerate.

Preheat the oven to 350 degrees. Remove the bread pudding mixture from the refrigerator. Butter the cups in a large muffin tin thoroughly. In a large mixing bowl, beat the egg white until it holds stiff peaks. Fold into the bread pudding mixture and mound the mixture in the buttered muffin cups. Place in the preheated oven and bake for 45 – 60 minutes until golden brown and cooked through. Yield: 12 "muffins."

Early in the twentieth century Saratoga's United States Hotel had on its wine list Chateau Margaux at three dollars a bottle and both Heidseck and Mumm's champagne at the same price. Good old days, indeed!

Here's a slightly less expensive way to serve your guests a refreshing drink. This recipe for **White Wine Punch** comes from Betty Powell, who says she has served it for years and it's always been a big hit. Instead of the white wine, you could use ginger ale for a children's party. To make the punch look festive, freeze fresh fruit like blueberries or finely cut-up

NEW YORK

WHITE WINE PUNCH

¾ **cup sugar**
½ **cup freshly squeezed lemon juice**
1 (40-ounce) can pineapple juice
1 quart white wine
1 quart club soda

Mix the sugar with the freshly squeezed lemon juice; stir until the sugar is completely dissolved.

Put ice in a large punch bowl. Pour in the pineapple juice, add in the sugar lemon juice mixture, and stir to blend. Add the white wine and the moment you are ready to begin serving, add the club soda.

Lawn jockeys salute at the entrance to Saratoga.

peaches in ice. If you have some small tin or aluminum molds, you can freeze the fruit in those. You can also use an ice tray. Start with a shallow layer of water in the molds or ice trays and when it freezes, add the fruit, fill up with water, and freeze again. It's easy to do and very impressive when served.

Menus from the United States Hotel for 1903 show us a wide selection but also reveal how tastes change. We don't relish pickled lamb's tongue or pig's feet, but we still enjoy fresh soft shell crabs, Boston baked beans, and roast loin of pork with fresh applesauce. Perhaps if we knew what "Spaghetti Mikado" was we might enjoy that as well. One simple dish that has survived from those menus to ours is creamed spinach. We have grown past the phase of having to be told to eat our vegetables, especially our spinach, and this is a simple-to-prepare, elegant accompaniment to almost any meal. **Creamed Spinach** is especially good with red meat.

A notation on the menu says a lot about the quality of what people were eating in 1903: "Vegetables fresh daily from United States Hotel farm." Unfortunately, back then chefs often overcooked those precious fresh vegetables to mush. Each menu also carries an impressive array of fruit preserves listed as a separate course. Many of these were probably made in the hotel kitchen from locally grown

---

CREAMED SPINACH

2 (1-pound) packages fresh spinach
3 tablespoons heavy cream
2 tablespoons butter
⅛ teaspoon nutmeg
Salt & freshly ground pepper to taste

Wash and remove any tough stems from the spinach. Chop. The packages usually say "Washed," but it needs to be done again unless you like sand as a piquant reminder of where your food originated.

In a large saucepan, over medium-high heat, cook the spinach, covered, for 3 – 5 minutes until it is all cooked down. You will have to stir it once to be sure all the leaves receive equal treatment and cook down. Remove from heat and drain. Return to the pan.

Put the butter in the pan with the spinach and stir to mix in. Add the cream and the "pinch" of nutmeg and stir. Serve at once, or put in oven-proof dish with cover and keep warm. Season to taste. Yield: 6 servings.

GINGERBREAD

1 cup molasses
1 cup sugar
¾ cup butter, softened
1 teaspoon ground ginger
2 teaspoons chopped candied ginger
½ teaspoon cinnamon
1 tablespoon grated fresh ginger
1 teaspoon baking soda
4 cups flour
2 eggs, well beaten
1 cup sour milk, or buttermilk

Preheat the oven to 350 degrees. Generously butter a 9x9x2" pan.

In a large mixing bowl, put the molasses, sugar, and softened butter together. Beat until well blended with a smooth, creamy texture. Sift together the spices, the baking soda, and the flour. Beat the eggs and milk together. Gradually beat in the flour mixture into the butter mixture alternately with the egg-milk mixture until all the ingredients are blended together. Beat the mixture until it is smooth and velvety, at least 3 minutes. Pour into the greased pan and put in the oven. Bake for about 50 minutes or until a cake tester inserted in the center comes out clean. Serve immediately with lemon curd or whipped cream dusted with powdered ginger. Yield: 9 generous servings.

NEW YORK

High-goal polo takes place at Saratoga in addition to racing.

fruit. That tradition has now come full circle with many of today's best restaurants having notations on their menus about produce and artisanal cheeses and other specialties they purchase from local vendors. Some restaurateurs and chefs have taken to bottling preserves, jams, vinegars, salsas, and other goodies and selling them at their restaurant and in local food venues.

Another of the items on the menu from the United States Hotel in 1903 that never went out of fashion is gingerbread. Maybe because it represents comfort food or maybe just because it tastes good all by itself with a tall glass of cold milk. For this volume we use an old **Gingerbread** recipe updated with the use of three gingers:

Gingerbread also keeps well. If it should become stale, simply slice each serving in half, toast it, and butter it. Instantly revived, it will bring to mind that old saying:

"May your good fortune spread

Like butter on warm gingerbread."

Polo, another activity at which Thoroughbred horses excel, was established in Saratoga in 1898. The Saratoga Polo Club has gone through many changes and has become one of the premier polo venues in the United States. The battle for the U.S. Polo Association's Monty Waterbury Cup, one of polo's top prizes, takes place here every August. Not so incidentally, the club also serves good food.

The Lily & Rose Catering Company does the food at the Polo Club, and this **Limed Avocado & Shrimp Salsa** is one of its most delicious offerings. Serve it exactly the way it is served at the Club: in a large martini glass, garnished with a dollop of cocktail sauce and one of the large cooked shrimp.

While few people are still capable of eating eight or nine courses, or would want to, good food is still very much a part of the Saratoga experience.

LIMED AVOCADO & SHRIMP SALSA

Juice of 2 limes
2 Haas avocados, firm & ripe
1½ cups cooked salad shrimp 150/200 count*
2 tablespoons chopped fresh cilantro
2 tablespoons extra virgin olive oil
Salt & cayenne pepper to taste
6 – 8 large, cooked shrimp to garnish
Cocktail sauce, optional

* Do NOT use canned shrimp, must be fresh.

Squeeze the limes; reserve the juice. Cut the avocado into ½-inch cubes. Make sure the shrimp are perfectly dry, pat with a paper towel if necessary, and add to the avocado. Toss gently to mix well. Sprinkle the cilantro over all. Whisk the olive oil and lime juice together, pour over the avocado shrimp mixture, and stir very gently to mix. Put mixture into martini glasses or other stemmed glasses, garnish each with a big shrimp and cocktail sauce if desired, serve. Yield: 6 – 8 servings.

CHAPTER

7

ILLINOIS

ILLINOIS

ARLINGTON PARK & THE MILLION

Noted poet Carl Sandburg called Chicago "hog butcher for the world." This was in the days when Chicago served as the gathering point for the Midwest farm belt's incredible bounty.

It was from Chicago that railroads headed east and ships headed north and east through the Great Lakes to eastern seaboard ports. Incoming waves of immigrants went West to work in the stockyards, mills, and factories and brought with them their old-country recipes and cuisine.

It was in Chicago that brick-oven pizza was first introduced. Italian immigrants spread along the lakefront, from Chicago north to Kenosha, Racine, and Milwaukee. This whole area of the country is infused with the richness of Italian culinary heritage plus that of many other countries.

All of this richness deserves a racing venue to match, and in Arlington Park, Chicago has it. Arlington Park has been referred to as the Taj Mahal of racing. If you haven't been there, the accolade might seem like an exaggeration; if you have been there, you wonder why you never thought of describing it that way. D. Wayne Lukas, who has seen plenty of racetracks, said that if you're going to introduce Thoroughbred horse racing to someone unfamiliar with the sport, Arlington is the ideal place to do so. And Jorge Velasquez, a jockey who rode regularly at Arlington, said it was the most beautiful track he ever saw. Those of us who have been agree. This is arguably the most beautiful, commodious racetrack in America. When it was rebuilt in 1985 after a disastrous fire, owner Richard Duchossois paid great attention to the comfort of the racing fan, and it shows.

The view of the track is unobstructed throughout the grandstand; there are six levels and not a bad seat in the house. The saddling paddock or enclosure can be seen from several

Arlington Park is arguably the most beautiful, commodious racetrack in America.

Racegoers can view the paddock from several levels.

levels. There is a large "classroom" right at the main entrance for those who have never attended the races and need to understand the arcane science of betting.

When you say "the Million," in Thoroughbred horse racing, everyone knows you mean the Arlington Million, the first race in the United States to offer a million-dollar purse. It doesn't seem so extraordinary now, but when the race was initiated in 1981, a million dollars was a lot of money for a racing purse. Run on Arlington's grass course, the race not only attracts the cream of America's turf horses, but has always drawn some of the best European horses as well. Arlington's very first race ever, in 1927, was won by a horse named Luxembourg, which might have been an indication of the future.

An American-born and -bred John Henry, though, won the inaugural Million. The gelding came from behind to beat the 40-1 longshot The Bart by a narrow margin. Actually, John Henry won the Million twice, the

Arlington created a special race for Cigar, who matched Citation's record of sixteen straight victories.

second time as a nine-year old in 1984.

Citation, Buckpasser, Dr. Fager, Native Dancer, Round Table, and Spectacular Bid have all raced at Arlington. Cigar came here to win the Citation Challenge and tie Citation's modern record of sixteen straight wins.

Churchill Downs Inc. has purchased a majority interest in Arlington from Duchossois, and as part of its plan to make Arlington once again a racing showpiece, it hired the Levy Corp. to attend to the food. The Levy Corp. first made its name with its showcase Chicago restaurant, Spiaggia. If you've been to Arlington and tried the **Arlington Park Gazpacho Soup**, it should tell you that the folk at the Levy Corp. know a thing or two about food.

ARLINGTON PARK GAZPACHO SOUP

1 cucumber, diced
2 green onions, sliced
½ yellow bell pepper, chopped
1 tablespoon chopped cilantro
¼ teaspoon minced fresh garlic
5 cups (40 ounces) canned tomatoes
⅛ teaspoon Tabasco® sauce or hot sauce

¼ cup fresh lime juice
¼ cup olive oil
1 teaspoon minced jalapeño
⅔ cup tomato juice
Salt & freshly ground black pepper
⅛ teaspoon cumin
⅛ teaspoon cayenne

Chop the cucumber, bell pepper, and cilantro, slice the onions, and mince the fresh garlic. Toss gently together to mix. Reserve.

Purée the canned tomatoes in a food processor. Put in a large, heavy-bottomed saucepan. Bring the tomatoes just to the boiling point and remove from the heat. Add the Tabasco®, fresh lime juice, and olive oil and stir to blend. Add the diced vegetables and stir again. Add the tomato juice, the salt and pepper, and the spices. Taste, adjust the seasoning, and chill before serving. Yield: 6 servings.

If desired, you can garnish each serving with a dollop of sour cream topped with chopped chives or more sliced green onion.

Even in an early incarnation, Arlington Park was expansive.

Gazpacho has become the summer soup of choice for many of us, as it is easy to prepare, tastes wonderful, and refreshes on a hot summer day. It's also low on calories, fat, and all the other things the medical community always warns us about.

Hot or cold, soup is a great way to feed people and an easy and forgiving dish to make. When I taught cooking classes, one of my favorites was the soups class. It was a favorite for two reasons: one, I have always loved good soup, and two, lots of men showed up to take the class. Usually they said something like, "I figured soup would be easy, and I'm spending too much money in restaurants." One of the soups I always "taught" is **Corn Chowder with Fresh Herbs & Country Smoked Ham** from the Prairie Restaurant in downtown Chicago, about a half hour from Arlington if the traffic's flowing.

Chowders are an American soup, originally made with fish, onions, and hardtack, a tough seagoing biscuit. Chowder appears to have been the creation of fishermen working the cold waters of the North Atlantic in the seventeenth century. Over time, butter, milk, and cream found their way into the mix, and then lean salt pork, and eventually clams.

CORN CHOWDER WITH FRESH HERBS & COUNTRY SMOKED HAM

1 tablespoon oil or bacon fat
2 russet potatoes, peeled, sliced thin
1½ cups canned corn with juice
1 medium carrot, peeled, sliced thin
½ small onion, peeled, diced fine
1 quart chicken stock*
1 cup heavy cream
1 chicken bouillon cube
1 bay leaf
**Fresh thyme, tarragon, and parsley
   tied up in cheesecloth (herb bouquet)**
2 canned pimentos, drained & diced fine
1 russet potato, peeled, diced in ½-inch cubes
2 cups canned corn, drained

Garnish:
   ¼ pound smoked ham, julienned
   **2 tablespoons chopped fresh thyme,
      tarragon, and parsley**
Salt & freshly ground black pepper to taste

* Homemade preferably, or the best quality you can buy.

Heat the oil or bacon fat in a large, heavy-bottomed pot. Add the sliced potatoes, corn and juice, carrot, and onion. Sauté for 5 minutes until the vegetables are slightly tender. Add the chicken stock, cream, bouillon cube, bay leaf, and herb bouquet. Bring to a boil, reduce the heat, and simmer.

Simmer for about 1 hour, or until all the vegetables are very soft and mushy. Remove the herb bouquet and the bay leaf. Purée in a blender or food processor until the mixture is smooth and velvety. Return the soup to the pot and add the pimentos, diced potato, and corn. Cook for another 30 minutes until the potatoes are tender.

Season to taste with the salt and pepper. Serve individually in bowls garnished with the julienned ham and the chopped fresh herbs. Yield: 6 servings.

ILLINOIS

The eternally popular gelding John Henry (outside) held off The Bart in the inaugural Arlington Million.

ARLINGTON'S SHRIMP & CRAB LOUIE

1 cup finely shredded Romaine lettuce
1 cup finely shredded white cabbage
8 (16/20-sized) shrimp, grilled
1 cup jumbo lump crabmeat
½ cup thinly sliced red onion
4 eggs, hard-boiled, peeled
8 asparagus tips, blanched
32 Kalamata olives
20 grape/yellow pear tomatoes

Dressing:
1 cup homemade or good mayonnaise
½ cup chili sauce
1 teaspoon finely chopped garlic
2 tablespoons red wine vinegar
½ green onion, finely chopped

For the dressing: Put all the ingredients in a small bowl and whisk briskly to blend well. Cover and refrigerate until needed. Shred the lettuce and cabbage. Put into a large bowl and toss with the dressing. Slice the tomatoes and the hard-boiled eggs in half. On each of four plates, mound the lettuce and cabbage. Place the thinly sliced red onion, the hard-boiled eggs, sliced tomatoes, asparagus tips, and Kalamata olives on top of the greens. Place the shrimp and lump crabmeat on top of the arranged vegetables. Yield: 4 servings.

Vegetables seem to have come last, as chowder moved away from the docks toward the farms. The first mention of corn chowder occurs in 1884 in Mary J. Lincoln's *Boston Cookbook*. Mrs. Lincoln was Fannie Farmer's predecessor at the Boston cooking school.

If you don't fall in love with this soup, its ease of preparation, and sheer deliciousness, then you're not a soup lover

For those who don't want to make the trip downtown, Ron Krivosik, the executive chef at Arlington, has come up with some appetizing fare for racing fans. For an appetizer or as a luncheon dish, try **Arlington's Shrimp & Crab Louie**.

One of the reasons I wanted to include Arlington in this book, in addition to its ambiance as a racetrack and a place to have a great time, was the chance to get back in touch with two men whom I regard as creative geniuses in the kitchen. I reached them both, and both

The first Arlington Million is immortalized in bronze.

ILLINOIS

GRILLED SESAME-MARINATED SPICY SHORT RIBS

5 pounds short ribs of beef
2 cups balsamic vinegar
1 cup brown sugar
½ cup vegetable oil
½ cup red pepper chili flakes
4 limes, zest & juice
2 tablespoons mustard seed
2 tablespoons coriander seed
2 tablespoons cumin seed
8 cloves garlic, peeled
1 4-inch piece fresh ginger, peeled
1 tablespoon salt
1 tablespoon cinnamon
1 ounce sesame seeds for garnish

To make the marinade, put the vinegar, brown sugar, oil, and all of the spices and seasonings together in the bowl of a food processor and process until you have a smooth purée.

Pound the meat of the ribs with a meat hammer until flat. Place ribs in a large non-reactive container (glass, ceramic, or stainless steel), cover with puréed marinade. Cover with plastic wrap and refrigerate overnight.

The next day start the grill. Once the grill is medium-hot, grill ribs, turning at least once, until they are cooked through, approximately 12 – 18 minutes.

Slice ribs between the bones into separate pieces. Pile ribs onto a platter and garnish with sesame seeds. Yield: 10 servings.

were enthusiastic about being in the book, saying it sounded like fun. With their recipes included, the food will be great, no doubt about that.

One of them, Tony Mantuano, owns a restaurant called Mangia in Racine, Wisconsin (not all that far from Arlington), in partnership with his dad. Tony has been the guiding force behind Spiaggia's success and has sent this recipe to tease the palate. Tony's wife Cathy, who is assisting him with a cookbook, says, "This recipe is from our Mediterranean restaurant Tuttaposto and was one of our most requested appetizers." Their recipe for **Grilled Sesame-Marinated Spicy Short Ribs** needs to be started a day before you want to serve it.

Make sure you have plenty of napkins when you serve this dish because you're going to need them.

Stephen Langlois provided me with another great pork recipe for this book. I met the young chef soon after he had opened his culinary sensation, Prairie. The restaurant, in downtown Chicago, on Printer's Row, was planned as a tribute to the architect Frank Lloyd Wright. While the restaurant was under construction, Langlois spent a year traveling the Midwest, visiting state fairs and historical societies, eating at local restaurants, and talking to people about food. When Prairie opened, the menu created major ripples in culinary circles. Steve had taken the best down-home farm recipes, and

GRILLED PORK CHOPS WITH BARBECUE BUTTER

For the barbecue sauce:
1 medium onion, peeled and quartered
3 cloves garlic, peeled
½ cup vegetable oil
1 (12-ounce) bottle dark beer
⅔ cup herb vinegar

1 cup light brown sugar, packed
⅓ cup Worcestershire sauce
1 (14-ounce) bottle chili sauce
1 (14-ounce) bottle ketchup
2 tablespoons barbecue spice

Combine the onion, garlic, and vegetable oil in a blender or a food processor fitted with a steel blade. Process until smooth, and transfer to a medium-sized saucepan.

Add the remaining ingredients to the mixture and stir well to combine. Bring the mixture to a boil and reduce the heat to a simmer. Simmer, stir occasionally, and skim off any foam that accumulates.

Let the sauce reduce by half, or until it is thick enough to coat the back of a spoon. Pass through a fine sieve or double layer of cheesecloth into a glass or other non-reactive container and refrigerate overnight.

For the barbecue butter:
2 cups unsalted butter, softened
½ medium onion, chopped fine
½ cup homemade barbecue sauce

½ teaspoon cayenne pepper
1 tablespoon Hungarian paprika
¼ teaspoon salt

Heat a small sauté pan over medium heat, and add 1 tablespoon of the butter. Add the onion and sauté until the onion becomes translucent but not brown, about 6 – 8 minutes. Remove from the heat and set aside to cool.

Place the rest of the butter in the bowl of an electric mixer or a food processor and whip on high speed until the butter is light and fluffy. Add the reserved onion, the barbecue sauce, cayenne pepper, paprika, and salt. Mix until well blended.

Lay out a 10-inch piece of plastic wrap on a flat surface. Mound the butter evenly along the edge of the wrap closest to you. Roll the butter up in the plastic wrap tightly to form a cylinder. Tie the ends of the plastic wrap, and puncture the wrap in a couple of places to release any air. Wrap the cylinder first in another layer of plastic wrap, then in aluminum foil and freeze overnight before using.

For the chops:
6 boneless, center-cut loin pork chops,
    1½-inch thick

Salt to taste
Freshly ground black pepper

Season the pork chops with the salt and pepper. Grill them over hickory chips that you've soaked in water, or cook them under the broiler in the stove. Because of the size of the chops, it takes quite a while for them to cook through — about 20 minutes. If they brown too quickly, simply wrap them in foil and put them in a 350-degree oven until they are cooked through. A meat thermometer inserted in the middle should read 160 degrees.

Arrange the chops on an oven-proof serving platter. Remove the barbecue butter from the freezer and remove the wrapping. Slice into ½-inch thick rounds and place 1 round of butter on each chop. Place under the broiler for approximately 30 seconds so that the butter just begins to melt. Serve immediately. Yield: 6 servings.

ILLINOIS

Turf racing, with its English and continental heritage, is an important feature at Arlington.

adding knowledge garnered at the Culinary Institute of America and during a couple of years cooking in Europe, brought to Prairie's tables some extraordinary dishes.

Grilled Pork Chops with Barbecue Butter is taken from the cookbook he did a year or so after the restaurant opened. You need to start a day ahead when you put together the home-made barbecue sauce and make up the barbecue butter the recipe requires.

This dish is not as much work as it seems. It is delicious and quintessentially American.

It should make you the hit of the bar-becue circuit. Midwestern farms are the major pork producers in the United States, probably in the world, so this dish definitely has its roots in Illinois.

A perfect complement to pork might be this unusual slaw from Arlington. Cole slaw is a term derived from the Dutch word *koolsla*, *kool* meaning "cabbage" and *sla* an abbreviation for salad. So cole slaw is cabbage salad. The term migrated to England where it was readily accepted since the English use the word cole to mean "cabbage."

A lot of American food goes better with a good cole slaw: barbecue, fried fish, bratwurst, hamburgers eaten outdoors, and even fried chicken on a

---

JICAMA COLE SLAW

2 cups shredded jicama
¼ cup chopped fresh cilantro
½ cup julienned, peeled English cucumber*
1 teaspoon chopped, seeded jalapeño pepper
½ cup julienned red bell pepper
½ cup julienned yellow bell pepper
½ cup julienned red onion

Dressing:
    ¼ cup good olive oil
    Salt & freshly cracked black pepper to taste
    ½ cup rice wine vinegar

* The English or European cucumber is long and thin and is now readily available in the produce department of most supermarkets.

Peel and shred the jicama; put in a large mixing bowl. Chop the cilantro and sprinkle over the jicama. Seed, peel, and julienne the cucumber; seed and julienne the peppers and add to the jicama. Peel and slice the onion thin to make julienne to match other vegetables. Add. Last, add the chopped and seeded jalapeño; toss to blend well.

Mix the dressing ingredients together in a small bowl and whisk briskly. Pour over the vegetables and toss to mix. May be made in advance and refrigerated. Yield: 4 – 6 servings.

---

picnic. Traditional cole slaw's basic ingredient is shredded cabbage. In this slaw, it's jicama. Since bratwurst, hot dogs, and hamburgers are on the Arlington menu, I bet they use a lot of **Jicama Cole Slaw**.

Jicama, according to the *Oxford Companion to Food* is "the underground tuber of a leguminous plant of Mexico." The Spanish spread this plant to other parts of the world in the seventeenth century, but it remains in widespread use only in the United States, southern China, and Mexico. It's a much under-utilized vegetable since it is easy to prepare, has a sweet mild flavor, and can be eaten raw or cooked.

Great Italian food abounds in the Chicago area. The Mantuanos are one family that is serious about its Italian heritage, most notably when it comes to the table. They always make their pasta fresh. So along with Tony's **Tagliatelle con Gamberi** (Tagliatelle with Shrimp

ILLINOIS

and Baby Zucchini) is their favorite recipe for making pasta. You can use a commercial tagliatelle if pressed for time.

Cathy Mantuano says, "We have tried many variations of pasta dough recipes, but have found this to be the best. This combination produces pasta with a firm, yet workable texture. Unlike for other

PASTA DOUGH

2 cups unbleached flour
8 egg yolks
1 teaspoon sea or Kosher salt
⅓ cup water

Pour the flour and salt in a mound on a pastry board. Make a hole in the center and add the egg yolks. Fold the flour over the eggs; add the water little by little, until you have a soft dough. Form the dough into a smooth ball, wrap in plastic, and let it rest, chilled, for one hour.

To roll and cut the pasta, cut a layer of dough off the ball, dust with flour, and place dough between the rollers of a manual pasta machine. With the rollers set the farthest apart they will go, pass the dough through. Fold the dough in half, sprinkle with flour, and roll again. Dust again with flour if the dough becomes too sticky. Continue this process, reducing the space between the rollers, one at a time until the dough is thin.

Generally, you can roll the dough 4 – 6 times on a setting before reducing the roller size until you are on the last setting, for which rolling twice will be enough. Let the pasta sheets dry for 5 minutes before cutting into tagliatelle or fettuccine.

TAGLIATELLE CON GAMBERI

2 tablespoons extra virgin olive oil
20 medium shrimp, heads on
½ cup cut up baby zucchini
2 cups lobster, shrimp, or vegetable stock*
1 pound tagliatelle or fettuccine pasta
4 tablespoons butter
4 leaves fresh basil
4 sprigs fresh chervil

* Lobster and shrimp stocks are available at seafood stores; vegetable stock can be purchased at most supermarkets.

Put a large pot of water on to boil. In a large sauté pan, sauté the shrimp in the olive oil until slightly colored on one side. Add the zucchini and the lobster stock and cook until the stock thickens slightly, about 10 minutes. Keep the sauce warm.

Cook the pasta in the now rapidly boiling water, until al dente, about 10 – 12 minutes. Drain well. DO NOT RINSE.

Add the pasta to the sauté pan. Add the butter and cook for 2 minutes or until the tagliatelle has absorbed some of the sauce. Divide the pasta, zucchini, and shrimp on warm plates, and garnish with the basil and chervil. Serve at once. Yield: 4 servings.

recipes, this pasta can be substituted for all types of pasta, thin tagliatelle, delicate ravioli, and even lasagna.

The only note from one of our testers was that the lobster stock she bought was so rich, she didn't think you needed as much butter as the recipe calls for in the sauce. That's a matter of individual taste, but Mary Jane's making it with less butter next time around, and yes, she's definitely making it again.

You now should be ready to take on the rest of the recipe for Tagliatelle con Gamberi.

The Mantuanos even offer advice on the best wine to serve with this dish. They recommend a Pinot Grigio, either Santa Margherita, from Trentino-Alto, Italy, or "El Dorado County" Edmunds St. John, California. They feel a Pinot Grigio is the perfect accompaniment for shellfish. Having tried it, I can only agree.

Another seafood winner is **Salmon**

SALMON WITH SUMMER TOMATOES IN LEMON VINAIGRETTE

For each serving:
1 (7-ounce) salmon fillet
Rice flour
Olive oil for sautéing
Salt & freshly ground black pepper
3 – 4 grape tomatoes
3 – 4 yellow pear tomatoes
1 – 2 plum (Roma) tomatoes
Fresh basil chiffonade*
Lemon vinaigrette:
    4 ounces fresh lemon juice
    Salt & pepper to taste
    4 ounces olive oil

* Chiffonade means to cut the basil in very thin slices crosswise. Do this just before serving to prevent the basil from discoloring.

Make the vinaigrette first. Combine the lemon juice and the olive oil; whisk briskly to emulsify. Add the salt and pepper to taste. Set aside.

Season the salmon with salt and pepper. Dip the salmon in the rice flour; shake off excess. Heat a sauté pan over medium-high heat and add the salmon. Cook, turning once to brown on both sides, for 10 – 12 minutes or until the fish flakes when tested with a fork. Remove at once and put on the plate with the tomatoes.

While the fish is cooking, cut the tomatoes into halves, wedges, or slices and arrange on the plate(s). Drizzle with the lemon vinaigrette. Place cooked salmon on top of the tomatoes and garnish with chiffonade of basil.

with Summer Tomatoes in Lemon Vinaigrette served at Arlington. Since salmon is now "farmed," good fish are readily available year-round. Try this dish at summer's peak when your garden is gushing tomatoes faster than you can use, can, or give away.

And after all that healthy food, think about your mental health and sit down to this unbelievably chocolatey dessert, called, appropriately, **Chocolate Brownie Sundae**.

The brownies initially are covered when you bake them and the tops appear shiny as

ILLINOIS

CHOCOLATE BROWNIE SUNDAE

8 ounces bittersweet chocolate chips
1½ tablespoons espresso crystals
8 ounces (2 sticks) unsalted butter
5 eggs
1½ cups sugar
1 teaspoon vanilla extract
1⅜ cups unbleached flour
⅜ cup Dutch-process cocoa
½ teaspoon salt
4 ounces bittersweet chocolate chunks
4 ounces milk chocolate chunks

Preheat the oven to 325 degrees. Liberally butter a 9x13x2" baking pan. Set aside.

In the top of a double boiler, over low heat, melt the chocolate chips and the butter. Stir together and when melted, remove from heat. Stir in the espresso crystals until well blended.

In a large mixing bowl, beat the eggs, sugar, and vanilla extract until ribbons form. Fold in the melted chocolate; blend thoroughly.

Sift the flour, cocoa powder, and salt together. Fold the dry ingredients into the batter; mix until they are fully incorporated. Fold in the chocolate chunks.

Pour the batter into the prepared pan and cover with aluminum foil. Put in the preheated oven and bake for 22 minutes; uncover and bake another 35 minutes or until a knife or cake tester inserted in the center comes out clean. Set aside to cool.

Cut the brownies into individual pieces and serve with white chocolate ice cream (or good vanilla ice cream) and hot chocolate sauce. Yield: 10 – 12 large brownies.

though still uncooked, but that's the desired effect. This batter makes a rich, fudgy brownie, a perfect foil for good ice cream and a homemade chocolate sauce. You could also top good vanilla ice cream with Grand Marnier for a more sophisticated sundae. Or use a premium coffee ice cream with the chocolate sauce.

A second dessert, **Sformato de Moscato d'Asti**, comes from the Mantuanos and is an easy, lovely dessert for a dinner party or adaptable for a family dinner. For the family simply substitute white grape juice for the sparkling wine.

Cathy Mantuano writes of this

CHOCOLATE SAUCE

4 ounces unsweetened chocolate
4 ounces butter
1 cup sugar
2 tablespoons 100% maple syrup

In the top of a double boiler, over barely simmering water, melt the chocolate and butter together. Remove from the heat and beat in the sugar until the sugar is dissolved and completely blended in. Add the maple syrup and beat again to incorporate completely. Keep warm until ready to serve.

(The maple syrup adds a shine and will keep the sauce from "breaking.")

dessert, "This was born out of the desire to serve our guests a dessert with simple, clean flavors. The sweet wine Moscato is fruity, low in alcohol, and refreshing. Quick and easy to prepare, this recipe is extremely versatile any time of year." I tried it with the white grape juice just to see how it worked, and it is delicious. And it is so easy to make. It takes about fifteen minutes to put it all together.

Cathy and Tony recommend serving these little treats with more of the Moscato d'Asti, but any good dessert wine would work equally well.

Chicago is one of the great restaurant cities in America. Cuisine from this "City of the Big Shoulders" is a wonderful mixture of all that is the melting pot that is America. A bonus is one of the premier racetracks in the world. If you live in the area and haven't visited Arlington, shame on you. Now that you know the food is wonderful and the horses some of the best in the world, you have no excuse.

SFORMATO DE MOSCATO D'ASTI
(WINE GELATIN WITH FRESH BERRIES)

6 (4-ounce) metal molds
2 cups Moscato sparkling white wine,* divided
⅔ cup sugar
2 packs of unflavored gelatin
½ pint fresh raspberries
½ pint fresh blueberries

* White grape juice can be substituted for the Moscato wine, if desired.

In a small saucepan, heat ½ cup of the Moscato until hot, but not boiling.

In a large mixing bowl, combine the heated Moscato wine with the sugar and the gelatin, stirring well to combine and melt the sugar. Let it sit for 2 – 3 minutes. Add the remaining Moscato wine and stir again to combine well.

Fill the molds two-thirds full with the fresh fruit. Ladle the gelatin mixture over the fruit into the cups until just below the rim. Refrigerate the cups until the gelatin is set and firm to the touch, approximately 2 – 3 hours.

To unmold, dip the molds into very hot water for 5 seconds and invert onto a plate. Garnish with whipped cream and additional fresh berries. You can serve the little gelatins on a bed of berry sauce, if desired.

Nectarines and peaches, peeled and finely cut up, can be substituted for the berries in season.

At Arlington, good horses and good food go together like an exacta.

CHAPTER

8

SOUTHERN CALIFORNIA

SOUTHERN CALIFORNIA

DEL MAR & SANTA ANITA

Southern California racing fans have it better than good. In addition to the wonderful climate, the Pacific Ocean right at their door, and the exotic vegetation, they have two of the most beautiful racetracks in the country.

Del Mar racetrack, just north of San Diego, has an ideal location. Where else can you sit in the grandstand and see the Pacific Ocean unroll at your feet? Feel the salt breeze as it comes off the ocean? Hear the waves as they crash on the shore? In Del Mar's early days, the horses used to be galloped on the beach.

With its incomparable locale, Del Mar has no trouble pulling in horse racing fans or top-notch horses. A couple of years ago, Tiznow, on his way to winning the first of two Breeder's Cup Classics, ran in the track's Pacific Classic and finished second to Skimming.

Del Mar is part of the San Diego County fairgrounds, where horse-related events take place year-round. Many residents of the Del Mar area are involved in the business in one way or another, including Rollin and Bonnie Baugh. Rollin Baugh operates a brokerage firm specializing in selling Thoroughbreds for racing and breeding. His services include appraisals, syndication, stallion seasons and shares, and mating recommendations. Although he maintains offices in Rancho Santa Fe, which is near Del Mar, and in Kentucky, Baugh's clients are geographically far flung with addresses in England, Ireland, France, Japan, New Zealand, Australia, and all over the United States. Some of the horses he's sold include Captain Steve, Phone Trick, Forty Niner, and Chief Bearhart.

Bonnie Baugh enjoys cooking and was enthusiastic about participating in *Racing to the Table*. She entertains often and shared her recipes for **Gravlox** and, in keeping with the location, her guacamoles and salsa. These are perfect recipes for your next Derby or Pacific Classic Day party. For the gravlox, you need to start a couple of days in advance. For the

Del Mar racetrack: "Where the surf meets the turf."

Going to the post at Del Mar on opening day.

BAUGH GRAVLOX

1½ pounds salmon fillet (tail section)

¼ cup Kosher salt

2 tablespoons sugar

1 tablespoon cognac

½ teaspoon freshly ground black pepper

Fresh dill sprigs

Mix the salt and sugar together.

Place the salmon on a large sheet of plastic wrap. Place the plastic wrap on a sheet of aluminum foil. Rub the salmon on both sides with the salt/sugar mixture. Wrap the salmon snugly first in the plastic wrap and then in the aluminum foil. Lay flat on a cookie sheet. Place another cookie sheet on top and use a five-pound weight to flatten out the fillet (a large cast-iron skillet or bricks will work). Refrigerate overnight.

In the morning, remove the fillet from its wrappings. It should have absorbed the salt/sugar mixture. If any is left, rinse off and pat dry with paper towels. Lay the salmon on a fresh piece of plastic wrap, rub the fillet with the cognac on both sides, grate the pepper on the fish, and lay a few sprigs of fresh dill on both sides. Wrap as before, put back on the cookie sheet, put the second cookie sheet on top, and weight as before. Let it sit overnight.

Remove from the wrappings. Slice as thin as possible on an angle as you would corned beef or flank steak. Serve on very thin pumpernickel bread with herb butter or cream cheese. The fish will keep for 1½ weeks in the refrigerator.

Herb butter:

1 pound unsalted butter

¾ cup minced fresh herbs (dill, chives, cilantro, etc.)

Juice of 1 lemon, with ½ teaspoon zest

Salt & freshly ground black pepper

Let the butter come to room temperature. Place in a mixing bowl, add the seasonings, and blend well. Cover and refrigerate until ready to use.

guacamole, you need to start about twenty minutes before your guests arrive.

Accompany the gravlox with one of the following **Guacamole** recipes. The word guacamole is not derived from Spanish, but from two Aztec words: *guaca*, which was the word for the avocado, and *mole*, which means "sauce." Salsa, including the recipe given here, can either be served on its own or added to guacamole. Bonnie advises wearing rubber gloves when seeding and mincing the hot peppers.

Salsa Fresca and Baugh's two versions of guacamole are a perfect prelude to **Marinated Tenderloin of Lamb**. This recipe begins with a marinade, and the meat is seared in a hot pan, though it could easily be grilled. Or you can simply go to Del Mar, hit the daily

SOUTHERN CALIFORNIA

Spanish Colonial details abound at Del Mar.

SALSA FRESCA

2 large, ripe tomatoes or 3 – 5 ripe plum tomatoes, finely diced
½ small onion, finely chopped
3 – 4 fresh jalapeño or Serrano peppers, seeded and minced
¼ – ½ cup chopped fresh cilantro
Salt & freshly ground black pepper to taste

Mix all the ingredients together in a non-reactive (glass, ceramic, or stainless steel) bowl. Refrigerate until needed.

double, and have Chef Christopher Logan make it for you.

Good fresh lamb is now available just about everywhere in this country. If your supermarket doesn't have a good meat department, seek out a butcher shop. It's worth the trouble if you're cooking something special like this.

The Pamplemousse Grille is so near Del Mar that you can almost see it from the grandstand. Its proximity also attracts the attention and patronage of the after-race crowd. Try the **Lobster Ravioli in Ginger-Soy Beurre Blanc** and you'll see why. Ambitious cooks can make their own ravioli pasta.

One of our testers wrote: "Something

GUACAMOLE I

2 avocados, one pit reserved
1 heaping tablespoon minced onion
½ teaspoon garlic salt

Gently mash the avocados, leaving them a bit chunky. Add the onion and garlic salt. Place the avocado pit in the center of the bowl and put the guacamole on top. Because this recipe does not use lime juice, the pit helps to keep the guacamole from turning brown. Serve immediately with corn or flour tortilla chips. Yield: Enough for 6 guests.

GUACAMOLE II

2 avocados, one pit reserved
2 – 3 heaping tablespoons fresh salsa (see earlier recipe)

Gently mash the avocados, leaving them a little bit chunky. Add the salsa and stir to blend well. Place the avocado pit in the center of the bowl; put the guacamole on top. Serve immediately with corn or flour tortilla chips. Yield: Enough for 6 guests.

MARINATED TENDERLOIN OF LAMB

1 (8-ounce) tenderloin of lamb

Marinade:
    ½ cup 12-year-old balsamic vinegar
    ¼ cup sweet rice vinegar
    2 tablespoons light soy sauce
    1 tablespoon ground cumin

½ teaspoon hot curry powder
¼ cup brown sugar
2 tablespoons finely chopped fresh garlic
1 teaspoon finely chopped Italian parsley
1 teaspoon finely chopped fresh basil
¼ cup sesame oil

Mix the vinegars with the soy sauce; add all the dry ingredients, the sugar, fresh herbs, and finally whip in the oil. Adjust the flavor to taste. Put the lamb tenderloin in a glass or stainless steel pan and cover with the marinade. Cover with plastic wrap and refrigerate overnight, turning once or twice to be sure all the lamb is marinated.

The next day preheat the oven to 350 degrees. Heat a pan and when hot, sear the lamb and place in the oven to finish to desired degree of doneness. For medium rare, you would want 160 degrees on a meat thermometer. This is a matter of minutes: 10 – 15 minutes, no more.

Cut the lamb on the diagonal and fan out on the plate. Serve with horseradish-whipped new potatoes. The lamb may also be served at room temperature on a bed of mixed baby greens as a salad. Yield: 1 generous serving.

SOUTHERN
CALIFORNIA

SOUTHERN CALIFORNIA

LOBSTER RAVIOLI
IN GINGER-SOY BEURRE BLANC

1 (2-pound) lobster
1 leek, halved and cut in thin half-moon pieces
2 tablespoons olive oil
1 teaspoon chopped shallots
½ teaspoon finely chopped fresh ginger
Salt & pepper to taste
1 tablespoon chopped, fresh tarragon
2 large shrimp, peeled & deveined
2 large scallops, membrane removed
1 medium egg
¼ cup heavy cream

Garnish:
   12 pieces asparagus, blanched
   12 yellow pear tomatoes
   12 red grape or pear tomatoes

For the lobster filling, first poach the lobster in boiling water for three minutes. Remove and cool. Put the olive oil in a sauté pan and heat, adding the leeks when the oil is hot. Sweat the leeks for 1 minute; then add the shallots, ginger, and salt and pepper to taste. Continue sautéing until the leeks are tender. Remove from the heat and add the chopped tarragon; stir to blend; set aside to cool. Remove all the meat from the lobster and dice into small pieces. Place in a colander to drain all the water from the lobster meat.

In a food processor, purée the shrimp and scallops. Add the egg and continue to purée until smooth. Remove to a mixing bowl and fold in the heavy cream. Add the cooled vegetable mixture and the drained, finely chopped lobster. Adjust the seasoning and refrigerate while you make the beurre blanc. Yield: 2 servings.

GINGER-SOY BEURRE BLANC

3 shallots, peeled, rough chopped
2 cloves garlic, peeled, crushed
6 peppercorns
¼ cup tarragon vinegar
¼ cup white wine
1 pound butter, cut in ½-inch cubes
1 teaspoon teriyaki sauce
1 teaspoon soy sauce
1 teaspoon peeled & finely chopped ginger

Put the shallots, garlic, peppercorns, vinegar, and white wine into a heavy-bottomed saucepan and reduce over medium heat until the liquid in the pan has the consistency of syrup. Watch carefully so it does not scorch. This will take 8 – 10 minutes.

Slowly whisk in the chilled butter cubes until all the butter is emulsified with the syrup. Add the teriyaki and soy sauce; whisk again to incorporate. Pass the sauce through a fine sieve; then add the ginger. Keep the sauce warm. It is important that the sauce not get too warm or too cool as it will "crack" or separate.

about the way the asparagus and lobster tasted together was heavenly…overall, the recipe was not too difficult to follow and was very tasty." She's going to use less butter and more ginger next time, but that's her personal taste. That's the fun of trying recipes like this one: loving it, but making it to reflect your personal tastes.

Next is a simple, quick, easy recipe for **Chicory & Kidney Bean Salad** submitted by Charlene Conway, who is married to comedian Tim Conway. To the racing world, Tim Conway is a hero, having founded the Don MacBeth Foundation with jockey Chris Mc-Carron and McCarron's wife, Judy. Started in 1987 to raise money for injured and disabled riders, the fund has raised millions to help injured and disabled jockeys. Mr. Conway, besides being a very funny man, is an exemplary racing fan.

RAVIOLI PASTA

9 ounces unbleached flour   **2 eggs**
¼ teaspoon salt   **3 egg yolks**
¼ teaspoon olive oil

Note: Instead of making your own ravioli pasta for the lobster, you can use wonton skins available at most supermarkets. Follow the package directions.

Put the flour, salt, and olive oil in a blender or food processor and process for a few seconds. Add the eggs and the extra egg yolks and process until the pasta dough begins to come together into a loose ball.

Turn the pasta dough out onto a lightly floured board and knead until the dough is smooth and even. Cut the dough into four equal parts and roll each into a ball. Wrap each ball in plastic wrap and allow the dough balls to rest in the refrigerator for 20 minutes.

Roll out one piece of the prepared pasta dough on a lightly floured surface; then feed it through a pasta machine several times until the pasta is as thin as an envelope. Using a pastry cutter, cut out four 4-inch circles and four ¾-inch circles. Spoon a good helping of the filling on each of the 4 smaller circles. Be careful to leave a clear edge around the filling to ensure a good seal. Brush the edges with a little water and top with the larger circles. Gently press the edges together. Using scissors, trim away any irregular edges of the ravioli. Gently pinch them all the way around to ensure the seal is sound. Refrigerate until ready to use. Use all the dough and all the filling in this way.

Cook in simmering salted water for about 3 – 4 minutes or until the pasta is al dente. Drain and keep warm as you plate the ravioli. Place some of the beurre blanc sauce on each of 4 plates; place several ravioli on each plate; cover with a little more of the sauce; then garnish with the asparagus pieces and the tomatoes. Yield: 4 servings.

SOUTHERN CALIFORNIA

Tim Conway

TIM CONWAY'S CHICORY & KIDNEY BEAN SALAD

2 heads of chicory or escarole, washed & trimmed
1 medium onion, peeled & sliced
1 (14-ounce) can red kidney beans
3 tablespoons olive oil
2 tablespoons red wine vinegar
Salt & freshly ground pepper to taste

Wash the chicory or escarole, discarding the tough outer leaves (unless you're an antelope). If you have a lettuce spinner, give the greens a few whirls.

Now pour the kidney beans and their liquid into a bowl and mash lovingly with a potato masher.

Put the chicory in a bowl and pour the kidney beans and their liquid on top. Add the sliced onion, olive oil, vinegar, salt and pepper, and then toss.

Serve this salad with pita, Italian, or French bread. Yield: 2 – 4 servings, depending on appetite.

Even in sleek, sunny Southern California, dessert tends toward comfort food. Two desserts, one from Del Mar, **Peach Cobbler Del Mar**, and one from the Pamplemousse Grill, **Strawberry-Rhubarb Crisp**, provide a soothing post-race finale to a racing meal. Both are fruit crisps, although Del Mar calls its version a cobbler. A crisp has a crumb-type topping while cobblers more typically have a biscuit-type topping. Either way both of these are well worth cooking and serving to family or friends.

Rhubarb is something my grandmother used to fix when she would visit us in the spring. I always associate rhubarb with spring, as it is the first fruit (it is really a vegetable that originated in southeastern Russia) of the season from the garden or available in the markets. Later it was combined with the first strawberries in dishes like this one. A memorable combination. Thanks to Jeff Strauss of the Pamplemousse Grill, you can start making some family memories of your own.

In Del Mar's early years horses exercised in the nearby Pacific.

PEACH COBBLER DEL MAR

2 cups frozen peaches, partially thawed
½ cup light brown sugar, packed
1 teaspoon vanilla extract
¼ teaspoon freshly grated nutmeg
1 tablespoon orange zest

Streusel topping:
4 tablespoons unsalted butter
¾ cup pastry flour
½ cup brown sugar
½ teaspoon cinnamon
¼ teaspoon freshly grated nutmeg

Preheat the oven to 350 degrees.

Use peaches slightly frozen; mix with the brown sugar, vanilla, spices, orange zest, and strawberry syrup. Add the melted butter and blend well; the butter should help bind everything together. Put the mixture in an oven-proof dish or in individual oven-proof ramekins.

For the streusel topping, put the cold butter, flour, sugar, and spices in a food processor. Process until the mixture looks like large peas.

Top the peach mixture with the streusel and place in the oven. Bake in the oven until the topping is golden brown and peaches are cooked but not mushy, about 35 minutes for large dish, 20 minutes for individual. Serve warm with premium-quality vanilla ice cream or top with slightly sweetened whipped cream. Yield: 4 servings.

STRAWBERRY-RHUBARB CRISP

4 cups rhubarb, peeled & cubed

4 cups strawberries, hulled & quartered

Zest from 1 orange

½ cup sugar

½ cup brown sugar, packed

1 tablespoon flour

2 tablespoons cornstarch

Peel and cube the rhubarb into a colander; then hull and quarter the strawberries into the colander on top of the rhubarb. Place the fruit in a large mixing bowl and add the orange zest, the sugars, flour, and cornstarch. Toss gently to mix.

Set out 6 individual ramekins or a 2-quart oven-proof dish. Preheat the oven to 375 degrees. Portion the fruit mixture out into the ramekins or put it all into the large oven-proof dish.

Crisp topping:

1 cup unbleached flour

4 ounces unsalted butter, cubed

½ cup sugar

⅓ cup brown sugar

1 tablespoon cinnamon

1 teaspoon freshly grated nutmeg

1 teaspoon salt

In a mixer with paddle attachment or in a food processor, combine all ingredients except butter. Mix thoroughly. Cut in cubed butter until moist. Be careful not to overmix. Spread on the tops of the individual ramekins or the large dish and place in the oven. Bake until the juices begin to seep out, or about 15 – 20 minutes for the individual crisps, and 30 – 35 minutes for the large dish. Yield: 6 servings.

This dish can be served with a good vanilla ice cream, a strawberry sorbet, or just plain whipped cream. It is best eaten warm from the oven.

SANTA ANITA AND THE BIG 'CAP

Santa Anita Park opened Christmas Day in 1934 in the middle of the Great Depression. Charles Strub came up with the idea of building a beautiful racetrack in a fabulous setting because he thought people needed and wanted distraction from their troubles. His intuition was on the money because they're still racing at Santa Anita.

Not content with just building a beautiful track in a wonderful setting, Strub initiated a race like no other. He created the Santa Anita Handicap, a race for horses three-years-old and up. But the real attraction, the attention getter, was the purse. In an era when top races carried purses of $6,000 and a $50,000 race was considered a fortune, Strub offered a purse of $100,000 for the Big 'Cap!

Seabiscuit added the 1940 Santa Anita Handicap to his impressive resume.

Although the huge purse was intended to attract attention and ease the pain of the Depression, Strub also wanted to lure the top Eastern horses to California. Remember that this was in the days when horses traveled long distances by rail, if they traveled at all. And to lure top East Coast horses to California, which meant a week-long ride in a boxcar, however luxuriously outfitted, you had to have a powerful attraction. The $100,000 purse did it.

Today's Santa Anita Handicap has a purse of one million dollars and serves as a showcase for the track's winter-spring race meeting. Innumerable great horses have won the

During its early years Santa Anita always packed a crowd.

race, from Seabiscuit to Spectacular Bid to John Henry.

Santa Anita has food worthy of the setting and the race. Try the **Parmesan-Crusted Chicken**, which comes topped with an arugula-tomato salad. It should convince you.

If after all that richness you're still hungry, Kristy Baugh has something you will definitely like. Kristy, the daughter of Bonnie and Rollin Baugh, went to cooking school so she is a pro. She shares her recipe for **Easy Chocolate Soufflés**. These small soufflés can be prepared ahead and kept refrigerated for up to six hours. So if you are going to make these for an elegant dinner party, plan on getting them in the refrigerator by early afternoon.

PARMESAN-CRUSTED CHICKEN WITH ARUGULA-TOMATO SALAD

3 tablespoons red wine vinegar

2 large ripe tomatoes, cut in 1-inch wedges

½ cup extra virgin olive oil

1½ cups julienned red onion

Freshly ground black pepper

4 (6-ounce) boneless chicken breasts, skin removed, lightly pounded

Salt & freshly ground black pepper

1½ cups unbleached flour

½ cup heavy cream

1 egg, well beaten

1½ cups Italian bread crumbs

½ cup freshly grated Parmesan cheese

¼ cup canola or safflower oil

3 cups cleaned arugula

Combine the red wine vinegar and the olive oil; whisk briskly to incorporate. Marinate the tomatoes and the onion in the dressing for 3 – 4 hours.

Lightly pound the chicken breasts so that they are of even thickness; then season with the salt and pepper. Set up a breading station: put the flour in a shallow bowl; beat the eggs and cream together in a shallow bowl; combine the bread crumbs with the Parmesan cheese and put the mixture in another shallow bowl.

Dip the chicken breasts first in the flour, making sure there are no wet or uncovered spots on the chicken. Then dip the chicken pieces into the egg wash, this time making sure there are no dry spots; the chicken should be completely coated in the egg mixture. Next, dip the chicken breasts into the bread crumb-cheese mixture. Use your hands; it's the only way to do this properly.

Preheat the oven to 350 degrees. Put a heavy-bottomed sauté pan on medium heat. When the pan is hot, add half of the oil and add the chicken breasts. Sauté until the chicken begins to brown and then turn over. Add more oil if necessary. When all the chicken is brown on both sides, place the pan in the oven and bake for about 15 minutes or until the chicken is cooked through.

Drain the tomatoes and onions, reserving the dressing. Toss the arugula with the reserved dressing; drain. Remove the chicken from the pan and let drain on paper towels. Place the chicken breasts on 4 warmed plates. Combine the tomatoes and the onions with the arugula. Mound the salad over the chicken a little at a time so that it stacks nicely. Serve immediately. Yield: 4 servings.

Then you can pop them in the oven while your guests sit down to the main course.

Racing fans equate Chris McCarron with the winner's circle, where until his recent retirement he frequently appeared atop some of the best horses in the world. Chris was one of the country's leading jockeys for many years. Like his fellow jockeys, Chris had to stay super-slim, which must have been difficult since he's married to a professional chef who owned a restaurant at one time. No doubt he is enjoying retirement and the new luxury of being able to eat as much of Judy's baking as he likes.

EASY CHOCOLATE SOUFFLÉS

6 (8-ounce) ramekins or small soufflé dishes

1 tablespoon unsalted butter, room temperature

1 tablespoon sugar for dusting

8 ounces good-quality bittersweet chocolate
6 tablespoons unsalted butter

1 tablespoon liqueur (optional) Grand Marnier,
**   Frangelico, or Kahlua**

6 large eggs, separated, at room temperature

½ cup sugar

Butter the ramekins, dust with the sugar, and set aside. Preheat the oven to 400 degrees.

In a heat-proof bowl over simmering water, melt the chocolate with the butter and, if using, the liqueur. Stir to blend until the mixture is smooth and completely blended. Remove from the heat.

In another bowl, whisk the egg yolks until they are light and lemon-colored. Add a little of the chocolate mixture and beat to incorporate. Then add the egg yolks to the chocolate mixture, whisking briskly to incorporate. Set aside.

In a large mixing bowl, using an electric mixer, beat the egg whites until soft peaks form. (A soft peak is one that droops slightly.) Add the sugar and continue beating until the whites form stiff peaks.

Stir ⅓ of the egg-white mixture into the chocolate, folding in gently with a large rubber spatula. Fold in the remaining egg whites in the same manner in two stages. Pour the batter into the prepared ramekins.

(If you are refrigerating the soufflés for later cooking, cover each one with plastic wrap and place on the lowest shelf of the refrigerator.)

Put the ramekins on the middle rack of the oven for about 20 minutes or until the soufflés are fully risen. Remove from the oven and dust the tops with powdered sugar. Take immediately to the table and serve with a small scoop of top-quality ice cream in the center of each soufflé. Or serve with just the powdered sugar dusting. Or a dollop of whipped cream.
Yield: 6 servings.

One of Judy McCarron's signature desserts is **Atea's Fresh Fruit Cake**. I used apples when I tested it in the fall. I intend to try it again in the summer using peaches or nectarines. It would also be wonderful with blueberries. (Judy's directions say to use any fruit but bananas.)

Chocolate chip cookies are as American as apple pie. There are almost as many variations of the cookie as there are of the pie. Judy McCarron's recipe makes a chocolate cookie that's almost a little cake. **Judy's Special Chocolate Chip Cookies** yield a very neat, good-for-a-party cookie, excellent for a cookie exchange, or just to serve with afternoon tea.

Newcomers to horse racing may wonder what becomes of a racehorse when its career is over, when age or infirmity dictates the wisdom of retirement. Many racehorses are retired to the breeding shed. Colts with great bloodlines and race records become sought-after stallions that hopefully pass along their abilities to their offspring. Many fillies become broodmares. But what of the geldings, those male horses that for whatever reason — lack of pedigree, rogu-

A statue of Seabiscuit has pride of place at Santa Anita.

ATEA'S FRESH FRUIT CAKE

2 cups finely chopped fresh fruit(s) skins on

1 cup finely chopped walnuts

2 eggs, room temperature, well beaten

1 teaspoon vanilla

2½ cups unbleached flour

1½ cups sugar

2 teaspoons baking powder

1 teaspoon baking soda

⅛ teaspoon salt

1 cup safflower or canola oil

2 tablespoons water

Chop the fresh fruit and the walnuts. Generously butter and flour a bundt pan or other ring pan. Preheat the oven to 325 degrees. Beat the eggs with the vanilla extract until the mixture is light and airy.

Sift the flour, sugar, baking powder, baking soda, and salt together into a large mixing bowl. Make a well in the dry ingredients and pour in the oil and the beaten eggs. Blend everything together, adding the water toward the end to help bind the dough together. Blend in the chopped fruit and walnuts so that they are evenly distributed throughout.

Put the dough into the bundt pan and press down to make sure the dough is evenly distributed all the way around. Put in the oven and bake for 1 hour; test with a cake tester to be sure the cake is cooked through. Remove from oven and allow the cake to cool before removing from the pan. Yield: 1 cake, 10 – 12 servings.

ish behavior — were neutered?

Some of those geldings go to retirement programs such as the California Equine Retirement Foundation (CERF). Programs such as CERF attempt to find second careers for horses that show suitability for jumping, other forms of competition,

SOUTHERN CALIFORNIA

Spectacular Bid won the Santa Anita Handicap as part of his undefeated four-year-old season.

JUDY'S SPECIAL CHOCOLATE CHIP COOKIES

10 tablespoons unsalted butter

1 cup dark brown sugar, packed

¾ cup sugar

1 egg, room temperature

1½ teaspoons vanilla extract

2½ cups unbleached flour

½ teaspoon baking soda

¼ teaspoon baking powder

8 ounces semi-sweet chocolate chips

1 cup chopped walnuts

Put the chocolate chips in the freezer at least one hour before you start making the cookies. In a large mixing bowl, beat the butter with the two sugars until the mixture is light and soft. Whisk the egg and the vanilla extract together and add into the butter mixture. Scrape down the sides of the bowl to be sure everything is incorporated. Sift together the flour, baking soda, and baking powder and add slowly to the butter mixture, scraping down the sides of the bowl as you beat in the flour mixture. You may have to blend in the last of the flour by hand, depending on the stiffness of the dough. Add in the chocolate chips and the chopped walnuts. Turn the dough out onto a sheet of plastic wrap, wrap tightly, and put in the refrigerator for 2 – 3 hours.

Preheat the oven to 325 degrees. Place the racks on the medium-high and medium-low positions in the oven. Generously butter 2 cookie sheets or cover with parchment paper. Remove the cookie dough from the refrigerator and shape the dough into 1½-inch balls and place about 1½ inches apart on the cookie sheets. Bake 8 – 12 minutes or until the cookies have risen and cracked. Do not overbake. Yield: Approximately 45 cookies.

or merely trail riding.

Grace Belcuore's CERF ranch has about seventy equine residents and a board of directors that reads like a *Who's Who* in California racing. When contacted for a recipe for the book, Grace, always thinking of the horses first, sent a recipe for the Christmas mash these retirees are treated to every holiday season. If you visit the ranch, which the public is invited to do on weekends, I bet you might find those great old guys (and a few gals) get a special mash more than just on holidays.

So if you have a horse, or friends who do, here's a special treat for them. And yes, we tested this recipe just as we did for all the others. The horses fed their first **CERF Christmas Mash** responded enthusiastically. There was not a single nay vote!

CERF's Christmas Mash

> **8 cups of bran**
> **1 cup of oats**
> **¼ cup vegetable oil**
> **¼ cup molasses (sometimes we use pancake syrup or honey)**
> **hot water (add until the mash is the consistency that you prefer. We use 2 cups)**
> **6 carrots sliced**
> **6 apples sliced**

Put the bran and oats in a large bucket; add in the vegetable oil, molasses, and hot water, and mix well. Add in the sliced carrots and apples and serve to enthusiastic diners.

Its elegant architecture and magnificent setting make Santa Anita the grandest of the California racetracks.

Index to the Recipes

BREADS

ENTREES

MEATS

FISH

INDEX TO THE RECIPES

DRINKS

MISCELLANEOUS

BIBLIOGRAPHY

Davidson, Alan. *The Oxford Companion to Food*.
(1999) Oxford, England: Oxford University Press.

Dean, Sidney W. *Cooking American*.
(1957) New York: Hill & Wang.

Editors of *American Heritage* Magazine. *The American Heritage Cookbook*.
(1964) New York: Heritage Press.

Langlois, Stephen, with Margaret Guthrie. *Prairie: Cuisine from the Heartland*.
(1990) Chicago: Contemporary Books.

Rawlings, Marjorie Kinnan. *Cross Creek Cookery*.
(1970) New York: Charles Scribner's Sons.

Van Nostrand, Elizabeth Riely. *The Chef's Companion: a Concise Dictionary of Culinary Terms*.
(1986) New York: Reinhold.

White, Jasper. *50 Chowders*.
(2000) New York: Simon & Schuster.

Women of Old St. Andrew's Parish Church. *The Tea Room Cookbook*.
2604 Ashley River Road, Charleston, SC 29414. Cost is $3.00 plus S&H.

There are many more cookbooks and books about food I have read over the past years that inform my writing about food, but these are the main ones used in compiling and completing *Racing to the Table*.

ACKNOWLEDGMENTS

No book, particularly a cookbook, is the work of one person. Without those "backstage," there would be no book. Their names are not on the cover, but their presence is vital:

Jackie Duke for having the idea and inviting me to do it; Chris Sobicinski of Delaware Park; Tony Terry at Churchill Downs; Dan Leary at Arlington; Mike Gathagan at Pimlico; Michele Blanco at Calder; Mac McBride at Del Mar; Charlotte Smith at Belmont; all the people at all the racetracks in this book who take the job of promoting racing very seriously, my deep gratitude.

Jan Waugh, the best point person one could ask for, Mary Jane Howell who played round 'em up at Dogwood Stable and tested every seafood recipe, and the folks at the Aiken Chamber of Commerce. Dr. Gary Norwood, who seems to know anyone connected with Louisiana racing who can cook. Anne McMahon, who knows everyone connected with New York racing and breeding.

All of the people who contributed recipes: Mike Wolken & staff at Keeneland; Mike Billows & staff at Saratoga and Belmont; Chef Conroy Smith & staff at Calder; the inimitable Ken Maceachron of Siro's, Gulfstream Park, and Santa Anita; Ron Krivosik, executive chef at Arlington and Churchill Downs; Craig Dennison and Pete deMarcay at the Fair Grounds; Christopher Logan at Del Mar; and all of the individual owners, breeders, veterinarians, jockeys' wives, bloodstock agents, and horse lovers whose names you will find attached to their recipes.

Joseph Pitta of the New York Historical Society; Ellen M. Shea at the Schlesinger Library at Radcliffe; Cathy Schenck at the Keeneland Library, all of whom are unfailingly helpful.

And the testers who, while not putting their lives at risk like the king's testers in medieval times, did yeoman service in making sure the recipes worked before they appeared before the cooking public. In alphabetical order: Terese Allen, a fellow food writer, trusted friend, and critic; Mark Blecher, who turns out to be almost as good at testing recipes as he is at fixing eyes; Mary Jane Howell; Donna Leegard; my sister Penny McCrudden who baked; Amy Schultz, an old friend and tester on three cookbooks; and my cousin Helen Fischer-White, who tested in a German kitchen, converting temperatures and amounts.

Any omissions have my deepest apologies and grateful thanks for working with me and helping to make this book the fun read I believe it to be.

Photo Credits

About the author

Citation, the last Triple Crown winner for the Calumet Farm power-house, made a racing fan out of Margaret Guthrie. Growing up in Philadelphia, the young Margaret kept a scrapbook with newspaper and magazine clippings of Citation's exploits on the track, including his record sixteen straight victories. She also learned to ride and remains a devoted equestrienne.

Guthrie's interest in food began when she was a teenager and continued after her years at Brown University. She has written numerous cookbooks, including the *The Best Recipes of Wisconsin Inns & Restaurants*, *The Best Midwestern Restaurant Cooking*, and *Quivey's Grove*. She collaborated on *Prairie: Cuisine from the Heartland* and *A Taste of the Northwoods*.

Guthrie's articles have appeared in *The New York Times Book Review* and its travel section, the *Christian Science Monitor*, the *Milwaukee Journal*, the *Philadelphia Inquirer*, and numerous magazines, including *Audubon*.

Guthrie, who has three grown children, lives in Philadelphia.

OTHER TITLES FROM ECLIPSE PRESS

At the Wire
Horse Racing's Greatest Moments

Baffert
Dirt Road to the Derby

The Calumet Collection
A History of the Calumet Trophies

Cigar
America's Horse (revised edition)

Country Life Diary
(revised edition)

Crown Jewels of Thoroughbred Racing

Dynasties
Great Thoroughbred Stallions

Etched in Stone

Four Seasons of Racing

Graveyard of Champions

Great Horse Racing Mysteries

Hoofprints in the Sand
Wild Horses of the Atlantic Coast

Horse Racing's Holy Grail
The Epic Quest for the Kentucky Derby

Investing in Thoroughbreds
Strategies for Success

Lightning in a Jar
Catching Racing Fever

Matriarchs
Great Mares of the 20th Century

Old Friends
Visits with My Favorite Thoroughbreds

Olympic Equestrian

Rascals and Racehorses
A Sporting Man's Life

Ride of Their Lives
The Triumphs and Turmoil of Today's Top Jockeys

Royal Blood

Thoroughbred Champions
Top 100 Racehorses of the 20th Century

Women in Racing
In Their Own Words

THOROUGHBRED
Legends®
SERIES

Affirmed and Alydar	Personal Ensign
Citation	Round Table
Dr. Fager	Ruffian
Forego	Seattle Slew
Go for Wand	Spectacular Bid
John Henry	Sunday Silence
Man o' War	Swaps
Nashua	War Admiral
Native Dancer	

EP
ECLIPSE PRESS

A Division of The Blood-Horse, Inc.
PUBLISHERS SINCE 1916